John Kirk

The Cloud Dispelled

John Kirk

The Cloud Dispelled

ISBN/EAN: 9783337346003

Printed in Europe, USA, Canada, Australia, Japan

Cover: Foto ©Lupo / pixelio.de

More available books at **www.hansebooks.com**

THE CLOUD DISPELLED:

OR, THE

Doctrine of Predestination Examined.

BY JOHN KIRK,

EDINBURGH.

WITH AN INTRODUCTION
BY
REV. DANIEL CURRY, D.D.

NEW YORK:
N. TIBBALS & CO., 118 NASSAU STREET.
PHILADELPHIA: LUTHERAN PUBLICATION HOUSE, NO. 42 NORTH NINTH STREET. BALTIMORE: T. NEWTON KURTZ, NO. 151 PRATT ST.

1860.

PUBLISHER'S PREFACE.

DURING the Session of the *General Synod* of the EVANGELICAL LUTHERAN CHURCH, at Pittsburgh (Penn.), in May, 1859, several of its clergymen boarded in a Scotch family, that called their attention to a work on PREDESTINATION, brought with them from their native land, and which they prized very highly. These ministers examined the book, and were so much pleased with it that they recommended its republication here. The family were unwilling to dispose of it, as they were not aware that another copy could be procured in this country. Several months afterward they agreed to part with the volume on condition that they should receive several new copies in return for the one in their possession, and accordingly it was mailed to New York.

The book, although published in 1847, presented a very venerable appearance, and looked as if it had been a product of the last century, so extensively had it circulated for perusal among the acquaintances of the family in Pittsburgh.

We are not aware that any work on this doctrine, of a moderate size, at a moderate price, and calculated for general reading, has been issued in this country, and by the publication of these Lectures we hope to fill a vacant place in our religious literature. The subject has been largely treated by theologians in their voluminous works, but they are beyond the reach of the masses.

These Lectures are written in such plainness of style that people generally can understand and appreciate them, while at the same time those who have read theology extensively can not but be attracted and instructed by their solid reasoning and strong common sense.

Hoping that they may *dispel the cloud* which has hung over the minds of many in regard to this much disputed subject, we present, with confidence, these Lectures to the judgment of an enlightened and discriminating Christian public.

New York, August, 1860.

INTRODUCTION.

It is somewhere remarked by that most acute and subtle of thinkers,—Coleridge,—that "had it been the object of the demon of dispute to invent a question in which all possible difficulties should be collected, it could not have been accomplished more to his heart's content than by starting this of Free Sovereign Grace." Setting out with a profession of special deference for the authoritative teachings of revelation, as compared with that of human reason and the intuitions of the understanding, the advocates of the doctrine of predestination proceed to build up that system by a process of strictly logical deductions. The recognition of the infinite Knowledge of God, comprehending as its objects, all things real and possible,—past, present, and future, is made to so occupy the mind as to exclude all practical apprehension of the other attributes of the Godhead, and to foreclose their influence upon the conceptions of the divine character and government. With this recognition of God's omniscience as a first premise, the argument proceeds by inferring the efficient pre-ordination of the things foreseen. Then to escape the appearance of a conflict between such an exercise of divine power with the principles and claims of justice, that attribute of God is degraded to a mere proprietary right,—the tyrant's power to do as he may please with his own. This view of the divine character is not only partial, and therefore monstrous, it is self-contradictory and self-destructive. God, as thus presented, is contemplated as a being possessing all knowledge, but without wisdom, and with all power but without love,—a blind omnipotence acting without a purpose or moral design. As thus considered, wisdom and goodness do not appear among the impelling and guiding influences by which the divine power is exercised: they are only the results of the relation of his acts to himself, and his acts are not performed by him, because they are wise or good, but they are so because he performs them.

The questions at issue between the advocates and the opposers of the doctrine of predestination are not likely soon to be settled. Both sides find abundant Scripture proofs in favor of their own peculiar views, but these proof-texts convey very

different ideas to different classes of minds. In
most cases of disputation upon the subject evidently the strife is simply about words, and in
not a few the whole subject is quite beyond the
mental grasp of the disputants. It is always
important that those who debate on any question should first ascertain in how far they are
agreed, and so to narrow the questions at issue
to those as to which there is a real disagreement.
As between the friends and the enemies of
the theological system popularly denominated
Calvinism, this precaution is often neglected.
With the former that system includes all the
great doctrines of salvation by grace,—so that
the doctrines of Original Sin, Justification by
Faith, and of Salvation by pure unmixed grace,
and by the sole merits of Christ's death, are
accounted distinctive elements of doctrinal Calvinism. And yet all of these are believed and
cherished by multitudes who reject the name of
Calvinists, and do not hold the distinctive tenets
of Calvinism. Between Calvinists and their
opponents the controversy is not about the doctrines of grace, but of predestination; though
the former strangely enough confound the two
together. To minds trained and habituated to
the modes of thought and the modes of inter-

pretation of Scripture that prevail among Calvinists, the Bible no doubt seems to be full of the doctrine of predestination : while to minds educated beyond the warping influence of an artificial and one-sided creed, the strongest proof-texts of the predestinarians are readily harmonized with the general teachings of the Bible, as these agree with the instincts of natural justice and righteousness in the human heart.

It is only just to concede to the advocates of the doctrine of predestination great praise for the clear and strong light in which they set some of the great doctrines of religion. From no other source do we meet with more just and worthy exhibitions of the majesty and glory of God, and of his awful Sovereignty. And from this view of the divine Majesty the mind passes naturally and almost necessarily to apprehend the guilt and vileness of sin, and the greatness of the work of redemption as to both the power and the price by which it is effected. But their fault is, that while thus exalting the divine glory in one of its aspects, they hide and becloud it in others equally important. The Almighty God is more than an awful Sovereign : He is also a tender and loving Father, delighting to do good to all His children. To contemplate the divine character without clearly recognizing this distinguishing glory of His name, is at once erroneous and damaging. God is indeed a Being of infinite majesty and dominion, and therefore He is to be feared and worshiped by all His creatures. He is also the Father of the Spirits of all flesh, —our heavenly Father, who knows and cares for all our wants—we may therefore confide in His goodness, and rejoice in His loving-kindness. And because the doctrine of predestination obscures these glories of the Godhead, it should be rejected as contrary alike to Scripture and reason.

The doctrine of predestination labors under the disadvantage of being opposed to the best instincts of our nature. It can not be denied that to most minds the notion, that the character and destiny of each individual are fixed by an eternal and irreversible decree, seems to make God unjust, and the whole array of exhortations, warnings and promises found in the Gospel, a mere mockery and cruel farce. It would, indeed, be harsh and unfair to hold those who accept that doctrine responsible for what to others seem to be its necessary implications; though the system itself must be held to such a responsibility. It is especially when brought to this test that the weakness of the system appears. Only let its opposers grant all that it claims, and then allow these assumptions to run onward to their legitimate consequences, and the system breaks down under the weight thus laid upon it. And this method of dealing with the subject is not only legitimate, it is the only one by which the question can be tested. As a subject of abstract reasoning, it is too vast and abstruse for our limited powers, and we can judge of it only by its relations to things which we are able to understand. We are more than authorized to reject any doctrine which dishonors God by contravening those eternal principles of justice, righteousness, and truth which He has implanted in our natures, and which we recognize as emanations from His own fullness. It is enough for us to know that our God will do right,—that He both punishes transgressors, and keeps mercy for thousands who love Him. In this aspect we delight to contemplate Him. The doctrine of predestination is, in the heart that receives it, a *cloud* dimming the brightness of the divine glory: but by the rising of the sun of Gospel truth *that cloud is dispelled,* and all men may see that *God is love.*

To aid in the work of *dispelling this cloud*

which an artificial and extra-Scriptural theology has interposed between men's minds and the divine glory, is the design of the following pages. Believing that undue claims to exclusive orthodoxy and to supereminent evangelism have been preferred in favor of those who embrace the doctrines of predestination, the Author has brought those doctrines to the tests of Scripture and reason, and has not only there stripped them of their false claims, but also convicted them of dishonoring rather than exalting the divine name. Here in a concise form the sincere inquirer after the truth may find the substance of the Calvinistic controversy presented with all requisite fullness, and its strange conclusions satisfactorily reversed. It is proper, and perhaps as should be expected, that Scotland, the land in which beyond all others the doctrine of predestination has had sway, should afford the needed antidote, and we are happy to present such a preparation in this little volume, to which the reader's attention is solicited, with the full conviction that its perusal can not fail to induce juster views of the divine dispensations, as harmonizing with the attributes of God, and with those principles of truth, justice, and goodness, which

He has implanted in men's hearts. With this conviction as to its relations and probable influences, is this little work now given to the American public, and with the earnest hope that under the blessing of God it may vindicate and diffuse His glory, and so contribute to the highest interest of His kingdom in the earth.

DANIEL CURRY.

NEW ROCHELLE, N. Y., Sept., 1860.

AUTHOR'S PREFACE.

Our God and Saviour is frequently represented in the Bible as a Sun—a glorious center of light and life. All who know Him are most fully prepared to acknowledge the appropriateness of the figure, and to yield their adoring affection to the attractive loveliness of Jehovah. Many there are, however, who "know not God," and who are perishing "for lack of knowledge." Error has taken the place of truth in their minds—error that covers the whole field of their spiritual vision, and shrouds the great and holy One in the deepest darkness. The experience of such is, that the less they think of Him the happier they feel. Very lately, I met with a most interesting person, who had been for many years in such a state of mind as to be unable to open a Bible, or listen to a word about God, without experiencing the most overwhelming horror. To a superficial observer, the experience of this person might have seemed the result of mental disease; but this idea is completely set aside by the fact that her suffering commenced by reading and hearing statements, that represented Jehovah as having, from all eternity, elected a portion of mankind, and as having reprobated the rest, while it was completely removed by the exposition of His true character. There are many such cases while there are many others in whom utter neglect of God is the result of this error regarding Him. The view given of His character and ways is of such a kind, as to appear an inextricable perplexity to their minds, and it is left in indifference as a subject on which they are not called to decide. Thousands are sinking into eternity who have no real hold upon the Rock of Ages, from these causes.

The object of this little volume is to dispel the erroneous conceptions that many have formed of Jehovah, in connection with the doctrine of predestination. The substance of what is thus published, having been delivered in a course of lectures, and several brought to rejoice in the Lord, through this means, it appeared desirable to give the exposition this more permanent form, that in the hand of the great Deliverer, the truth might be useful to a much wider circle than could otherwise be reached. Deeply conscious of the imperfection of the effort so far as I am concerned, but confident in the truth and in that God whose honor I have sought to vindicate, I commend these pages to Him, and to the careful consideration of my fellow-men.

J. K.

Edinburgh, 1st June, 1847.

CONTENTS.

LECTURE I.
PREDESTINATION AND THE FOREKNOWLEDGE OF GOD. . . 17

LECTURE II.
PREDESTINATION AND THE WISDOM OF GOD 40

LECTURE III.
PREDESTINATION AND THE JUSTICE OF GOD 56

LECTURE IV.
PREDESTINATION AND THE TRUTH OF GOD 73

LECTURE V.
PREDESTINATION AND THE LOVE OF GOD 87

LECTURE VI.
PREDESTINATION AND THE CRUCIFIXION OF JESUS . . . 105

LECTURE VII.
PREDESTINATION AND GOD'S PURPOSE IN JESUS 117

LECTURE VIII.
PREDESTINATION AND THE WICKEDNESS OF MEN . . . 129

LECTURE IX.
PREDESTINATION AND THE STUMBLING OF MEN 143

LECTURE X.
PREDESTINATION AND THE INFATUATION OF THE REPROBATE 152

LECTURE XI.
PREDESTINATION AND THE HARDENING OF HEARTS . . 172

LECTURE XII.
PREDESTINATION AND THE DEATH OF THE REPROBATE . 198

LECTURE XIII.
PREDESTINATION AND A FOREORDAINED JUDGMENT . . 217

LECTURE XIV.
PREDESTINATION AND THE BOOK OF LIFE 233

LECTURE XV.
PREDESTINATION AS FOUND IN THE BIBLE 247

LECTURE XVI.
PREDESTINATION AND THE SECURITY OF BELIEVERS . . 261

LECTURE XVII.
PREDESTINATION AS A FOUNDATION OF HOPE 274

THE CLOUD DISPELLED.

LECTURE I.

PREDESTINATION AND THE FOREKNOWLEDGE OF GOD.

The subject of discussion on which we are now entering is one of no trifling moment. If we regard it in the light of a doctrine that has been woven into the very texture of the mind of our country—that sways the feelings, and influences the consciences of vast multitudes of our fellow-men—it must appear worthy of most serious and earnest attention. Or, if we regard it as most vitally affecting the character of our God, its claims upon our consideration are incalculable. Let us, then, in the spirit of those who seek truth for its own sake, for man's sake, and for the sake of the honor of our God, enter on, and pursue this momentous subject.

You are probably aware that the Catechism which we, and millions of others, have committed to memory from our earliest years, contains the doctrine, that "the decrees of God are His eternal purpose, according to the counsel of His will, whereby, for His own glory, He hath foreordained whatsoever comes to pass." This is a plain declaration, that God has foreordained "WHATSOEVER COMES

TO PASS." This doctrine has taken a deep hold upon the minds of men. When a crime is committed by persons who are held deeply guilty before God, nothing is more common than the saying, "It was before them, and they could not get past it." A friend of mine, on entering a company, some time ago, had occasion to state, that on the night before, a man had committed suicide in the most fearful manner. What effect did the relation of this worst of crimes produce upon one of the oldest and apparently most serious of the company? Simply this: She exclaimed,—" Poor man, his time was come." Such was the principal feature in the case, as it appeared to her mind, and such is the legitimate conclusion from the doctrine, that whatsoever comes to pass is foreordained. Many have thus imbibed the doctrine of a universal predestination, while many others, of more reflective minds, stumble over it, and are thus effectually prevented from seeing the true character of their God. These considerations, then, ought to weigh heavily with us, in leading our minds to the test of eternal truth, on a subject that has taken a position of such importance. First of all, it is right that I should state clearly the doctrine which I mean to bring to the test. It is not that there is such a thing as predestination. I believe that many events that have come to pass have been decreed to take place by God. The doctrine to be considered is that of UNIVERSAL PREDESTINATION—the doctrine, that WHATSOEVER COMES TO PASS IS ETERNALLY FOREORDAINED. This is the doctrine which has been quoted from the Catechism, and which leads men and women to say of crime committed by them,—"It was before us, and we could not get past it;" and it is this doctrine that hides from many an inquiring mind the true glory of the character of Jehovah. It is this doctrine, therefore, that must be brought to the test; and I shall endeavor to do so by bringing *saving* truth to bear on it, so that, while we reason on predestination, the mind may be led into the riches of "the glorious gospel of the blessed God."

As it is necessary, in an inquiry of this kind, to begin at the foundation of the subject on hand, our attention is first called to the relation in which the doctrine of universal predestination is supposed to stand to the foreknowledge of God. This is stated by a living author of no small influence, as follows: "The question is, does God fix a thing simply because He foreknows it? or does He foreknow it because He has fixed it? There are vague ideas in men's minds on these points, and it is well to know the truth with distinctness. I answer, then, unhesitatingly, that predestination must be the foundation of foreknowledge. God foreknows EVERYTHING THAT TAKES PLACE BECAUSE HE HAS FIXED IT." * Nothing can be more explicit than this; and if God HAS FIXED EVERYTHING, the persons who say of their own crimes, or the crimes of others, "they were before us, and we could not get past them," are perfectly right. It is impossible that they could get past that which God had fixed for them. A man with whom I conversed some time ago, went to his minister with the difficulty of election or predestination upon his anxious heart. After a good

* Truth and Error. By H. Bonar.

deal of explanation, which still left the man's mind in the same state of darkness, he asked the minister if it did not, after all, come to this: that if he had been elected, he would be saved, and if not, his salvation was impossible? The minister replied, that however inconsistent it might appear to their minds, it did come to that. It must, then, be carefully marked, that in the doctrine of universal predestination, there is distinctly involved *the predestination of sin*, as well as of life and death. Indeed, this is distinctly stated by the author before us. He says:—"Here is something still more striking. The deeds of these wicked men (the murderers of Jesus) are said to have come to pass according to his counsel." Again, "They teach us plainly, that our world's history, in all its things, great and small, is a history of events preordained by God from eternity." If this be true, then again we say that those are right, and in no error, who say of *their crimes*, "they were before us, and we could not get past them." At present, then, our desire is to call earnest attention to this doctrine, as it is supposed to issue out of the Bible truth of the foreknowledge of God. The great, and, in many cases, insuperable difficulty of the mind is thus stated. God, by His omniscience, foreknows everything that comes to pass. He can not foreknow that which is uncertain, therefore all is fixed. In this chapter, I shall call attention to two important branches of reasoning; First, to the scriptural denial of the foreordination of sin; and, Second, to the fallacy by which that false doctrine is founded upon the omniscience of God.

I. The scriptural denial of the doctrine that Jehovah has foreordained iniquity.

It may be thought strange, by many readers, that we should require to produce formal scriptural proof on such a subject as this; yet, let it be remembered, that if sin be not foreordained, then, "whatsoever comes to pass" is not foreordained; and the theory, that God foreknows everything because He has fixed everything, is a false theory. It is thus of vital importance to our argument to see that the Bible repudiates the whole doctrine, by repudiating that part of it which has respect to sin.

1. *Consider the words of God in Jeremiah* vii. 29-31 :. "Cut off thine hair, O Jerusalem, and cast it away, and take up a lamentation on high places; for the Lord hath rejected and forsaken the generation of His wrath. For the children of Judah have done evil in my sight, saith the Lord, they have set their abominations in the house which is called by my name, to pollute it; and they have built the high places of Tophet, which is in the valley of the son of Hinnom, to burn their sons and their daughters in the fire; which I commanded not, *neither came it into my heart.*" Now, let us suppose that "whatsoever comes to pass" is foreordained by God, and then we must admit that these sins of Judah were foreordained by Him. These sins " came to pass." How does this theory look in the presence of Jehovah's most solemn protestations in the verses now quoted? Mark, he tells Jerusalem to cut off her hair, and to cast it away in token of deep and desperate grief. Why should she do this? Is it be-

cause that has come to pass which Jehovah decreed? Is she to exercise inconsolable grief, because the eternal determinations of her God have not been counteracted and rendered a failure? How is it possible for men to credit the affirmative of such a monstrous question? But, further, the Lord is said to have *rejected* and *forsaken* the generation who committed, or brought to pass, these things; and He designates them "the generation of His wrath." Are we, then, to believe that they became the people of His indignation, and were rejected and forsaken *because* they brought to pass that which had been decreed by Himself from all eternity? To such a question we must reply in the affirmative, if it be true that everything that "comes to pass" is fixed to be as it is by the eternal decree of God. The author who says that God foreknows everything that takes place, because *He has fixed it*, and who thus holds that God fixed from eternity that Judah was to commit the sins spoken of before us, holds that that generation were rejected and forsaken as a generation of wrath, because they did that which God from eternity had fixed to be done! Now, my reader, can you believe this? Are you prepared to declare that such doctrine is the truth of God? If so, how can you feel sorry for sin? How can you feel remorse for having fulfilled the eternal decree of your God? How can you regard that God, when you see Him rejecting, and forsaking, and eternally punishing men for doing that which He Himself irrevocably decreed to be done? You must feel difficulty in allowing your mind to rest for a moment in the contemplation of such a character as professedly divine. But observe further, Jehovah says that He commanded not these things. This may be admitted. Well, He goes further. He says that "*they came not into His heart.*" Can you still hold that He had them in His heart from all eternity, as the things which He determined, and fixed to take place for His own glory? I know it is possible to bind the mind to the reception of any idea, however absurd it may be, by saying, "it is spoken after the manner of men." Let us, then, apply this theory to the case before us. Let us suppose that a man's family are completely under his control, so that he can make them do exactly what he chooses. Well, he determines that a portion of them shall furnish him with an opportunity of condemning and punishing them, that he may display what he calls his justice. In order to this, he decrees secretly that they shall commit the most horrid crimes, and as they do commit these crimes, they are just carrying out his own determinations. What would you think of the "*manner*" of the man who, in such a case, would protest, in the presence of his condemned children, that the sins they had committed had never entered his heart? Most unquestionably you would hold his manner to be that of a devil, and not of a man. How, then, can you venture to ascribe to God such a "*manner*" as this? Yet you must either do so, or forever abandon and condemn the doctrine that He has "foreordained whatsoever comes to pass." I dwell upon the solemn declaration of Jehovah, because nothing but the omnipotence of divine truth itself will meet the tenacity with which men cling to the idea, *that all is foreknown, because all is foreordained.* It is an idea that is regarded by multitudes as an *axiom*—as a truth that no *sane* man can dispute. We confront it, therefore, by the solemn words of God Himself, as He flatly contradicts it. But we must proceed to the passage that is parallel to that now considered.

2. *Take the words of Jehovah in Jeremiah* xix. 1-6: " Thus saith the Lord, Go and get a potter's earthen bottle, and take of the ancients of the people, and of the ancients of the priests; and go forth into the valley of the son of Hinnom, which is by the entry of the east gate, and proclaim there the words that I shall tell thee; and say, Hear ye the word of the Lord, O kings of Judah, and inhabitants of Jerusalem; thus saith the Lord of Hosts, the God of Israel, Behold, I will bring evil upon this place, the which whosoever heareth, his ears shall tingle. Because they have forsaken me, and have estranged this place, and have burnt incense in it unto other gods, whom neither they nor their fathers have known, nor the kings of Judah, and have filled this place with the blood of innocents; they have built also the high places of Baal, to burn their sons with fire for burnt-offerings unto Baal, which I commanded not, nor spake it, neither came it into my mind: therefore, behold the days come, saith the Lord, that this place shall no more be called Tophet, nor the valley of the son of Hinnom, but the valley of slaughter." This is a still stronger passage than that in the seventh chapter of this prophet. It is important to notice some of its most striking features. The prophet was directed

to take "a potter's earthen bottle," to represent the people and the city to whom he was to address himself. After speaking to them the words of Jehovah, he was to break the bottle in pieces before them, as a sign of the fearful judgment with which God would punish the iniquities which they had committed. God said that He would bring evil on the place, that whosoever heard of it his ears should tingle. He said emphatically— "*they have forsaken me.*" This could not mean anything less, or else, than that they had forsaken His friendship and His laws. They could not escape from His presence. He says further, "they have *estranged* this place." How could they estrange it but by using it contrary to His purposes regarding it. If they did all that they effected in accordance with His eternal decree, how could they be justly said to have estranged the place? But mark what He says respecting their crimes—" which I commanded not, nor spake it, *neither came it into my mind.*" It is impossible for Jehovah, as a holy and sin-hating God, to speak in stronger terms than these. With the man who values the word of his God above the *axioms* of his own reason, the question must be settled here. When He says that the sins *came not into His mind*, to say that, notwithstanding this declaration, He fixed that they should take place, is to contradict Him in the plainest possible manner.

We shall have occasion afterward to consider other passages of Scripture containing a similar denial of the doctrine in question. Let these suffice at present. It is better that the mind should have the full advantage of two such decisive protests, on the part of God, than that it should be led to feel as if *many* such were *required* in order that they might prove conclusive. When Jehovah says, respecting a series of events, that they *came not into His mind*, the man that still insists that He ordained them to take place for His own glory, may say anything else. He is assuredly proof against every thing like the force of divine authority in the Bible. O, my hearer, remember that it is no trifling matter to have such a declaration as that now before us to contend with. It is no slight sin to set aside such a solemn denial of having anything to do with evil, when that denial is made by the living God. "Heaven and earth shall pass away, but His words shall not pass away." They will come up in judgment at last, and confront those who have set them aside, and if any word must thus appear in judgment, it must be that before us. It was at the hour of judgment to the guilty Israelites that it was first uttered. Let us, then, feel the weight of these passages against the supposed axiom, that whatever is foreknown is fixed of God to take place.

II. Consider the fallacy upon which the doctrine of the foreordination of sin is founded.

The mind may be placed in great difficulty by a mere scriptural *denial* of a particular doctrine—it may not have been accustomed to bow with implicit submission to the words of the Bible; or it may have been under the power of that most misleading of all notions, that the Book of God contains doctrines that *must* appear to us contradictory. Although, to such a mind, you produce the strongest assertion, from the Word of God, disproving a particular doctrine, the man is not led to abandon the doctrine thus disproved. It is needful, therefore, to point out the flaw that vitiates the doctrine in question, and exposes it to the denial of God.

1. *Let us have the doctrine again clearly before us.* The substance of it is this,—that because it is admitted that God foreknows whatsoever comes to pass, and because He could not have foreknown it unless He had fixed that it should take place, therefore God foreordained every thing that comes to pass, and that from all eternity. A correct idea of the doctrine may be derived from the argument founded upon it in the following conversation. It is supposed to be here presented in a light in which it is unanswerable. "If I am not mistaken," says the author, from whom I quote, "the conversation related took place more than half a century ago. It is, however, very suitable as an illustration of some of the points discussed in the preceding pages. The chief speaker was a minister of an Independent congregation. Being once on a journey, he was overtaken by a stranger, who urged some objections to predestination, and, among others, that it made God unjust.

"'Before that can be admitted,' said the minister, 'you must prove that God owes eternal life to any of His fallen creatures; and further, that the vindication of a mortal is essential to the equity of a God. Besides, the question is not, what are the difficulties connected with the doctrine, or can a worm solve them all?—but, is this doctrine of predestination scripturally and philosophically true, or is it not? The difficulties of the subject will prove nothing against the fact; and he that brings the legislation of his Creator before the tribunal of his own understanding, should first be able to measure the length of His eternity, the breadth of His immensity, the height of His wisdom, and the depth of His decrees. Is it not a sad evidence of human depravity, that creatures of a day will sit in judgment on spiritual and eternal things, as if the Author of the great mystery of godliness were altogether such an one as themselves?'

"'I hope you will not be offended,' replied the gentleman, 'if I declare, notwithstanding all you advance, I do *not*, I *can not*, believe in this doctrine of predestination.'

"'And I hope,' rejoined Mr. C., 'that you will not be offended if I declare I am quite of opinion you *do believe* in it.'

"'I beg, sir,' said the other, 'you will explain yourself.'

"'If you will favor me with the short answer of Yes or No, to a few explicit questions I shall take the liberty to propose,' replied Mr. C., 'I have little doubt but I can prove what I have affirmed.'

"'It will afford me great satisfaction,' said the other, 'to comply with your proposal.'

"Mr. C. then began: 'Are you of opinion that all sinners will be saved?'

"'By no means,' said the gentleman.

"'But you have no doubt,' added Mr. C., 'it

will be formally and finally determined, at the day of judgment, who are to be saved, and who are to perish?'

"'I am certainly of that opinion,' replied the stranger.

"'I would ask, then,' continued Mr. C., 'is the great God under any necessity of waiting till these last awful assizes, in order to determine who are the righteous that are to be saved, and the wicked who are to perish?'

"'By no means,' said the other, 'for He certainly knows already.'

"'When do you imagine,' asked Mr. C., 'that He first attained this knowledge?'

"Here the gentleman paused, and hesitated a little; but soon answered, 'He must have known from all eternity.'

"'Then,' said Mr. C., 'it must have been fixed from all eternity.'

"'That by no means follows,' replied the other.

"'Then it follows,' added Mr. C., 'that He did not *know* from all eternity, but only *guessed*, and happened to guess right; for how can Omniscience *know* what is yet uncertain?'

"Here the stranger began to perceive his difficulty; and after a short debate, confessed it should seem it must have been fixed from eternity.

"'Now,' said Mr. C., 'one question more will prove that you believe in predestination as well as I. You have acknowledged, what can never be disproved, that God could not know from eternity who shall be saved, unless it had been fixed from eternity. If, then, it was fixed, be pleased, sir, to inform me who fixed it?'

"The gentleman candidly acknowledged he had never taken this view of the subject before, and said he believed it would be the last time he should attempt to oppose predestination to eternal life."

In many minds this is supposed to be an invincible argument; and many an inquirer has been silenced and left in inextricable difficulty when plied with it, as this gentleman was.

2. *Let us see now where the strength of the argument lies.* This will be seen in the virtual assertion contained in these words, "How can Omniscience *know* that which is uncertain?" Study carefully the whole conversation, and you will find that if Omniscience may, or *can know,* that which is yet uncertain, the whole argument, and every argument of the kind, falls to the ground. The minister virtually asserts that even God *can not* foreknow an event which is yet uncertain; and here, and here *alone,* has his argument a resting place. Take this away, and it is gone. Show that Omniscience *may* know of the coming of an event, without Omnipotence *fixing* that event, and so rendering it *certain,* and the whole boasted fabric crumbles in an instant into dust. It is important to notice this most carefully. Nothing can be of greater moment in dealing with an argument that contradicts God, than seeing most clearly the assertion upon which it rests. This is of special importance in this instance, because the assertion is so manifestly of a suspicious nature—"OMNISCIENCE CAN NOT KNOW!" These are suspicious words—words that can not be

reflected on without exciting a degree of suspicion in regard to the assertion in which they occur. What is it, we are apt to ask, that OMNISCIENCE CAN NOT KNOW? What does omniscience mean? Does it not mean ALL-KNOWING? What is it that an all-knowing mind CAN NOT know? The assertion is that it CAN NOT know "that which is yet uncertain." Well, here is the peg upon which the whole matter hangs: that which is supposed to be a perfect axiom in defense of predestination as universal, is the simple assertion that God Himself CAN NOT know the coming of an event unless He has first fixed that it shall come.

3. *Let us now test this assertion.* It is not so self-evident, nor is it so clear a quotation of the Bible, that it may not be questioned and put to the test.

(1.) It proves too much. It is used to prove that eternal life is a subject of predestination. It is also used to prove that the act of God in condemning the wicked is predetermined. But mark well, my hearer, that it proves, as certainly, the predestinating of *every sin* as that of either eternal life or condemnation at the seat of final judgment. If God can not know that which is yet uncertain, and thus must have fixed all that He knew would take place, then every lie, and theft, and murder, that have ever been committed in time, must have been *fixed* of God to take place, and that from all eternity. Then, we say again, that the statement of the criminal, " it was before me, and I could not get past it," is true. The argument either proves this, or it proves nothing. If the crime of the murderer might be foreknown without being fixed, then every thing else may. Hence, there is not even the *shadow* of consistency in those who deny the eternal predestination of sin, and yet use this argument. God foreknew the sin—the assertion is that He can not foreknow that which is not fixed, and in eternity no one could have fixed the coming events but Himself. Thus it is made to appear that He fixed every sin that ever was committed, to be committed just as it is, so that a crime is just the result of God's eternal decree as truly as any thing possibly can be! When will the blinded mind see the horrid nature of such a doctrine as this? Look closely to it, my hearer, and ask your own soul if there must not be something wrong with an assertion that, if admitted, inevitably proves the predestination of every sin, and that by a sin-abhorring God?

(2.) The assertion in question is contradictory in its own terms. This I have already noticed as giving ground for suspicion in regard to it. I notice it now more particularly to show that it is false. Observe, then, the word OMNISCIENCE. It means THE POWER OF ALL-KNOWLEDGE, or the power in God of knowing ALL THINGS. The assertion is, that if any thing is "*yet uncertain*," this power in God CAN NOT take it in—that Jehovah, though possessing the power of INFINITE knowledge, CAN NOT know an event which is yet uncertain. Now, this is plainly saying that the power of the divine mind to know is infinite, and yet it is finite—that it is capable of knowing all things, but not capable of knowing an uncertain event. I can not see how it is possible for an assertion more fully to contradict itself.

(3.) The assertion measures divine knowledge by the standard of human knowledge. We are not sure but it gives less power to the knowledge of God, than must, in right, be granted to the knowledge of man. Even man may know, and that with a feeling of the most perfect certainty, how events, yet future, will occur; and yet these events may be entirely beyond his control, and suspended upon the fickle will of his fellow-man. But we insist not on this. Even if we admitted the impossibility of human knowledge grasping with certainty the future occurrence of an event which is yet left perfectly uncertain, does it follow that we must transfer this incapacity to know of such an event to the knowledge of God? By no means. Man is less than nothing and vanity, when compared with God; and though it were impossible with man, that would be no reason for supposing it so with God. The person who first uttered the question, "how can Omniscience *know* that which is yet uncertain," no doubt felt that HE could not know such events; but it was too much to conclude, therefore, that God could not know them.

Here it is most important to remark, in passing, that the word "*uncertain*" is an ambiguous word, and hence apt to mislead the mind, when used in such a question as that under consideration. It is very generally used to signify that of which we are as yet ignorant. For example, an event has occurred in a foreign land, and the news takes months to reach this country. Two persons meet to converse over the state of things abroad. One asks the other how some particular events have gone. The other answers, that no news has as yet arrived, and adds, "As yet, all is *uncertain.*" Here he uses the word concerning events that have actually taken place. He calls them "*uncertain,*" because the truth regarding them has not yet reached the public mind. Were the word used in this sense, in the assertion that God can not know that which is uncertain, the statement would simply mean, that He could not know that which He did not know. But this is not the meaning of the word. It is not used in opposition to knowledge, but to fixedness.* Contingency, therefore, being the only other meaning of it, to this we must recur. The assertion is, that God can not know an event, or foreknow it, if it actually possesses the nature of a *contingent* or *unfixed* occurrence. In this meaning alone, it has force in the argument before us; and again we hold, that had not man presumed to limit and pare down the power of Jehovah's knowledge to the level of the standard of his own, he would never have asserted that God could not foreknow an event which is in its nature perfectly *contingent.*

(4.) The assertion in question is founded in the most dishonoring ideas of God. I pass at present the notion that He predestinated sin. I leave also the idea, for the next lecture, that He *can not* create a free creature, whose actions shall be perfectly

---

* "Necessity is that which is, and which can not possibly not be, or be otherwise than it is. Contingency, then, as the opposite idea, must be *that which is, or may be, and which possibly might not be, or might be otherwise than it is.*"—*Tappan.*

contingent events. That upon which it is needful to insist here, is the idea, that if an event were truly contingent, God could not know that event before it took place. This idea is admirably opposed by John Goodwin in his valuable work, "*Redemption Redeemed.*" There he says,—" If it be replied, yea, but if God knows that such and such things will come to pass, is there not a necessity of their coming to pass; or otherwise, must not the knowledge of God prove abortive, and be accompanied with error?

"I answer, no; if the events supposed to be known by God before their coming to pass be contingent; or, at least, such, in the production whereof, the wills of men must some way or other interpose, if ever they be produced (of which kind of events only we now speak), the certainty of the knowledge of God may be saved, and yet no absolute necessity of the coming to pass of such events be supposed. The reason is, because at the same time when God seeth or knoweth, that they will come to pass, He seeth and knoweth also, that there is no necessity they should come to pass, but that they may well be prevented, in which respect, in case they should not come to pass, the knowledge of God should suffer no defeature or disparagement.

"If yet it be said, yea; but, when it is supposed that God knoweth that such or such an event will come to pass; if it should be supposed withal, that He knoweth it may not come to pass, or that it may come to pass otherwise than according to His knowledge, doth not this suppose or imply a consciousness in God of the weakness or deficiency of His knowledge?

"I answer no; but rather the contrary; viz., a consciousness in Him of the strength and perfection of His knowledge. For he that knoweth not that contingent and free-working causes, which way soever they shall act in order to any particular event, might yet act otherwise, or suspend their actings, is certainly defective in knowledge. And if God did not as well know that there is a possibility of the non-futurity, or of the not coming to pass of such contingent events, which He knoweth will come to pass, He should be defective in His knowledge concerning the nature and property of contingent and free-working causes, inasmuch as this is their nature and property (as hath been said), to be at liberty, in reference to particular actings, to act one way as well as another, or else to suspend their action. Indeed, if it should be said or thought, that any event *will* not, or *shall* not, come to pass, which God knoweth beforehand will come to pass, this would import an obnoxiousness unto error in the knowledge or foreknowledge of God. But to say, or think, that such an event, whose future coming to pass God knoweth *may*, notwithstanding this knowledge of His, not come to pass, reflects no dishonor or disparagement at all upon His knowledge, but rather gives an honorable and high testimony of excellency and perfection unto it. For he that certainly knows what contingent and free-working causes will do, notwithstanding their freedom and liberty either to do, or not to do, or to do otherwise, must needs be excellent in knowledge indeed, and one who needeth not count it robbery to be equal with God." This is a true and striking exposition of the doctrine of the divine glory of foreknowledge. We are here enabled to form some true conception of the almighty power of Divine Omniscience, while we are relieved from the freezing and deadening notion, that everything is fixed, as by inexorable fate, and yet we have the full advantage of the soul-cheering truth, that "all things are naked and open to the eyes of Him with whom we have to do." We are here also enabled to see the real shallowness of the pretended *depth* of those who advocate the glory of God through the doctrine of universal predestination. We are also enabled to see the true bearing of such ascriptions of praise as can be rendered to God, on the ground, and in the spirit of this doctrine. It is a praise that had much better be withheld, and for which we can not conceive of God as looking upon His creatures with less than profoundest pity and disapprobation. The very foundation of the doctrine, so far as foreknowledge is concerned, is the assertion that God *can not* foreknow an event, unless He has first of all fixed it irrevocably, and takes care that it shall come to pass. Who sees not that this assertion robs Jehovah of glory. It is founded on robbery of God. Under the pretense of exalting Him beyond the stretch of the mind of men, it drags down His excellency to a level with that of man, and even beneath it. We have in this assertion a remarkable instance of the real dishonor that is done to the name of God under the idea of doing Him honor.

4

4. *Let us now see the truth that requires to be admitted, in order to the entire removal of this whole argument from foreknowledge.* One would suppose that some most fearful error must flow in, if universal predestination is denied. From the zeal with which that doctrine is defended, we might conclude that the whole fabric of truth must be overturned if it is even *partially* set aside. Now, all that needs to be admitted is, that GOD CAN CREATE BEINGS WHOSE ACTIONS SHALL NOT BE FIXED EVENTS, AND YET THAT HE CAN FOREKNOW WHAT THOSE ACTIONS SHALL BE. We have thus before us the truth, and how can any reflecting man object to it? Let me ask my hearer, if he will rather admit that all sin has been foreordained by the decree of God, and that Omniscience *can not* know an event which is yet uncertain, than he will admit that God can create a creature whose actions shall be truly contingent events, and yet the whole of whose history shall be perfectly foreknown of God? Weigh the alternatives, and you can not be in a difficulty as to which to choose.

In closing this lecture, let me press with deep earnestness the fact of freedom on the mind and conscience of my hearer. Are you still without God as the object of your supreme delight? Are you still afraid to think of meeting Him? Could He now point to you and say, "there is at least one that loves me not?" O! my fellow-sinner, He has created you free—He has not fixed one choice of your undying mind—He could not value your choice if He had, for forced love is an abomination alike to God and to man. You are free, and free to look to Him as your Father and eternal Friend—free to meet Him on the ground that Jesus atoned for your sins—free to enjoy Him as your eternal portion. Dare you think of the fact that you have freely chosen the world, and rejected God? Remember, those theories that seem to prove that your sin has been a fixed matter from eternity, will be swept away by the tide of the indignation of the God of truth at last. "The hail shall sweep away the refuges of lies." O! then be entreated to choose now the free and full mercy of your God. Be entreated to rest on the fact that Jesus atoned for your deep and voluntary criminality. Be satisfied with that which honors and satisfies divine justice. Be reconciled to Jehovah, and you will bless Him throughout eternity that He created you free, and redeemed you from the curse you had chosen, that you might freely choose everlasting life.

LECTURE II.

PREDESTINATION AND THE WISDOM OF GOD.

MANY suppose that the admission of the doctrine of the foreordination of whatsoever comes to pass, is essential to the honor of divine wisdom. An author whom we have already quoted writes as follows:—" For an infinitely, wise, holy, and gracious Being to arrange everything according to His own wisdom, holiness, and grace, appears to us the very perfection of things." By "everything," this author means every sin as well as everything else. It is thus supposed that in order to the "perfection of things," we must grant the foreordination of everything by God. Thus, the doctrine which we have seen so emphatically renounced by God Himself, is regarded as essential to the honor of His wisdom.

In this lecture, I shall endeavor to show two things—first, that divine wisdom is vailed by the doctrine of universal predestination; and second, that it is magnified by the doctrine of the real freedom of man. Let it be strictly marked that the doctrine with which I contend includes the foreordination of sin. To this I would earnestly beg the special attention of the hearer. If sin is not foreordained, the whole argument about foreordination is lost; for if sin may take place without foreordination, so may other events that depend for their occurrence on man's free will.

I. The wisdom of God is vailed by the doctrine of universal predestination.

There are several things necessarily deemed essential to a character for wisdom, of which the doctrine in question deprives the character of God. In mentioning and illustrating some of these, it will be seen that even man would justly spurn as a disgrace that which is ascribed to God as an honor.

1. *Divine wisdom will always act in a transparent manner.* The conduct of God must be such as to be easily seen through, so far as its rectitude and benevolence are concerned. Now, it is the uniform confession of those who ascribe the predestination of all things to God, that they can not vindicate His conduct. They hold decidedly that it is *not* transparent conduct—yea, that the friends of God, enlightened by His Spirit, are not to expect to be able to vindicate it. An author of this class writes as follows: "Other theories undertake to explain and vindicate the divine administration, to the satisfaction of human reason—with what success, let the tendency from one expedient to another in the attempt to get rid of mystery show. This, alone, frankly owns the impossibility of making all plain; and takes its appeal to the undoubted supremacy and almighty power of God as the only answer, in the last resort, to caviling questions; and all the service it pretends to render is, that it assigns to the inexplicable knot its right position."* Such is the confession—nay, such is the boasted excellency of the system to which the doctrine of the predes-

* Dr. Candlish on the Atonement.

tination of all things belongs. It speaks of the vindication of God's ways to man as "*impossible*," and regards the conduct of Jehovah with man's will as an "inexplicable knot." What do we think of the man whose conduct is incapable of vindication? Do we think him wise, or holy, or gracious? Hear further confession on the same point. Another author says—" I believe that the invitations of the gospel are to all without exception. Yet, while I believe this, I believe in election too. 'Many are called but few are chosen.' If I am asked, How can you reconcile these things? I answer that I am not careful to reconcile them, I am satisfied that God has told me that *both* are true."* Here, then, is first a declaration of the *impossibility* of vindicating the ways of God to men, and then a cool confession of indifference on the point. These are the inevitable results of the doctrine in hand. "*Impossible*," and "*careless*," are words that indicate the very states of mind, in regard to the vindication of God, which this doctrine must naturally produce. Now, it is of considerable moment—ay, of *infinite* moment—to ask if God treats His own vindication in this style. Does He admit that it is impossible to vindicate His ways, or does He profess indifference as to this vindication? Read His words and you will see. Isaiah v. 3–4: "And now, O inhabitants of Jerusalem, and men of Judah, judge, I pray you, betwixt me and my vineyard. What could have been done more to my vineyard that I have not done in it?" Mark the position which God takes up in this passage. He

* Truth and Error.

puts the sinner—the unbelieving sinner, too—in the seat of the Judge, and bids him decide upon the treatment which he has received. Contrast this with the miserable confession that we have just noticed. In the one case the advocates of God confess, that it is *impossible* to vindicate His ways to the satisfaction of human reason; in the other, Jehovah puts that very reason in the seat of judgment, and bids it decide upon His ways. Which of these modes of acting show the greatest wisdom? Whether is it evidence of almighty skill so to act, that even an *enemy* may be called upon to judge of what is done, or to act so that even a *friend* must confess that it is impossible to vindicate the course pursued? The question is its own answer. Well, is not divine wisdom turned aside and driven to hide itself, because of the doctrine in question? O! my hearer, do not judge of your God by such a view as this. Let His own clear and unquestionable ways be judged. He Himself appeals to you, and prays you to give that judgment; and nothing but the wretched system that declares the foreordination of sin, could dismiss His appeal by saying,—"It is impossible to vindicate His ways."

2. *Divine wisdom will always be able to clear itself from all share in bringing about the crimes of men.* If God, from all eternity, "*fixed*" every event that takes place, then He must have "*fixed*" every *sin* that takes place. If He *fixed* that I should sin in each instance in which I have sinned, —if He determined, before I existed, that these sins should be committed, how is it possible to hold

that He is entirely free from all share in the existence of these sins? This is the very question which, it is acknowledged, it is impossible to answer. Now, does this indicate wisdom on the part of God, if it be true that sin is foreordained from eternity? According to this doctrine He has made an arrangement, and part of that arrangement is, that men should commit sin, and furnish Him with an opportunity of displaying His indignation in punishing that sin; but that arrangement is not of such a nature as to make it clear that He is not, after all, the originator, and the cause why sin is committed! O! it is deplorable to what extremes men will go when prepared to admit that it is impossible to vindicate the ways of God to men. Still, it is most important to mark, that the doctrine in hand shuts out the wisdom of God from the view of those who adopt it. They hold Him to be wise—they assert that He is wise, but they do not, and can not see wisdom stamped upon all His procedure. With them it is not clear, like a sunbeam of heaven, gilding with glory the plan of Jehovah. No, all is *dark—inexplicable*—incapable of vindication—incapable of clear and Godlike separation from the abominable deeds of the sinner. How different the ways and the vindication of God Himself! He shows, on every occasion, that sin is *strange* to all His desires, purposes, and designs—that it is the accursed intrusion of the guilty upon the holy arrangements of His great universe—that it is abhorred in His deepest heart, to be expunged from all that He holds dear, and swept at last into the place of *outer* darkness.

3. *Jehovah's wisdom does not need sin that He may thereby glorify Himself.* The whole doctrine of universal predestination proceeds on the idea, that sin was needed in order to the fullness of divine glory. This will be seen very clearly in the following words:—" I grant, indeed, that all the children of Adam fell, by the will of God, into that state of misery wherein they are now bound. God did not only foresee, but He did dispose the fall of man, and in him the ruin of all his posterity. The first man fell, because God so judged it to be expedient; why He so judged it is unknown to us, yet it is certain that He so judged it for no other reason but because He saw that thereby the glory of His name should be worthily set forth." * The doctrine of these words is, that God needed sin in order to the full glory of His name. This is further clear in the answer given by another author to the question—" Did God make men to damn them?" The answer is not as it ought to be, a stern denial of the infamous imputation, but as follows:—" God made man—every man and every thing—to glorify Him. This every creature, man or angel, must do either actively or passively, either willingly or unwillingly—actively and willingly in heaven, or passively and unwillingly in hell." † These are the words of a man who believes that God can only foreknow that which He has fixed from all eternity. The doctrine is clearly this, that God made arrangement for sin and hell, that by means of these He might more honor Himself by mercy and justice in redemption and condemnation. Now, we may well

---

* Calvin's Institutes. † Truth and Error.

ask the question—is this honoring to the divine wisdom? Would it be honoring to a father if he felt it needful to arrange so as that his children should be abominable profligates, and many of them perish, in order that he might be honored in pardoning and punishing? We hesitate not to affirm, that the arrangements of such a father would be felt to be infamous, rather than glorifying; from the very foundation they would be felt to be so. The arrangement and ordination of the sin would infinitely counterbalance the mercy, and deprive the justice of all but the name—ay, even of the name itself. The very case in hand is a striking proof of this. When we ask as to the justice and mercy of God in dealing with sin which He *fixed* to take place, and that in the counsels of eternity, we are told that it is *impossible* to vindicate His ways to human reason. Now, is that *glorious* which it is *impossible to vindicate?* Is that what men understand as *glorious*, which even the friends of the doctrine *confess* they can not reconcile with justice and mercy, and regarding which the best they can say is, that *it is so*, and, therefore, must be *just?* We have different conceptions of glory; so has every man; and the idea that God's infinite wisdom needed *sin* to promote His glory is truly miserable. It is well exposed in the following words:—"For doubtless God is not so poorly or meanly provided, in and of Himself, for the exaltation of His name and glory, as to stand in need of the dunghill of sin to make a footstool for Him whereby to ascend into His throne." * The system that represents His

* Goodwin, p, 80.

glory as in any way depending on sin is mournful. It is clear, then, that the doctrine of predestination vails the wisdom of God, inasmuch as it represents that wisdom as failing to vindicate its own ways—as failing to show its entire freedom from all fellowship with the sinner in the production of sin, and as requiring the wretched abominations of the sinner in order to promote its own glory. Divine wisdom, indeed, is, by this doctrine, converted into the most fearful species of cunning—that cunning that requires and uses the crimes of others to effect its own aggrandisement. If it is supposed by my hearer that this is too strong language, let him read the following words of the great Apostle of predestination :—" Though none receive the light of faith, nor do truly feel the effective working of the gospel, but they that are foreordained to salvation, yet experience showeth that the reprobate are sometimes moved with the same feeling that the elect are, so that, in their own judgment, they differ nothing from the elect. Wherefore it is no absurdity, that the apostle ascribeth to them the taste of the heavenly gifts, that Christ ascribeth to them a faith for a time; not that they soundly perceive the essential force of grace and assured light of faith; but because the Lord, the more to condemn them and make them inexcusable, conveyeth Himself into their mind, so far forth as His goodness may be tasted without the spirit of adoption."* Reflect, my hearer, upon that passage, and ask your own soul if you would not shrink with horror from the course of conduct that is thus ascribed to God; and

* Calvin's Institutes.

yet this is supposed to indicate the perfection of wisdom. Perish forever the doctrine that ascribes such wisdom to God. O! let us turn to the opposite view, and see how the truth glorifies Jehovah.

II. THE WISDOM OF GOD IS MAGNIFIED BY THE DOCTRINE OF MAN'S TRUE FREEDOM OF WILL.

We have been contemplating a doctrine that requires the acknowledgment that it is impossible to vindicate the ways of God to the satisfaction of human reason; and the two parts of which, its most devoted votaries are despairingly *careless* to reconcile. Let us see if the doctrine of man's perfect freedom of will requires any such acknowledgment and carelessness.

1. *Divine wisdom is glorified in the creation of a creature* TRULY FREE. What an amount of divine majesty is expressed in these few and simple words of God: "Let us make man in our own image, after our own likeness, and let them have dominion." There are two ideas most manifestly essential to the right understanding of these words,—first, how could man have the image of God if all his actions were *fixed* by an irreversible decree before he was made? and second, how can man be said to *have dominion* if he was only the machine carrying out the inevitable decrees of another? Is the moral image of God *possible* in that mind, every volition of which is determined by a previous necessity? Why, instead, in such a case, of bearing the image of God, man would bear no moral image at all. Not one of his determinations would originate with

himself,—they would merely be the effects of the determinations of another. This would destroy the very idea of morality in his case; and the idea of *dominion* in such a situation as this would be a simple mockery. *Man* can bring into existence a machine to act as he determines it; but Jehovah can create a free spirit to determine its own choice —to sit in the throne of dominion; and surely in this there is a display of the most incomprehensible wisdom. The creation of a spirit—intelligent, immortal, and free, bearing the stamp of Divinity itself, and fitted to occupy a throne,—this is a work worthy of Him whose wisdom is unsearchable. The more glorious the work as a work of God, the greater, surely, is the glory that is due to Him whose work it is. What a contrast between the wisdom that pre-determines sin itself, in order to have an opportunity of pardoning one and condemning another, and that of the Creator calling into existence an undying spirit, so gloriously constituted and free! Surely, if we can form any conception of the very essence of holiness itself, and see that holy conduct must be *free, spontaneous,* and *voluntary,* we see the perfection of skill and wisdom in Him who makes a spirit capable of that holiness. Such is the honor accruing to the wisdom of God from the truth of man's real freedom of will.

2. *Divine wisdom is glorified in the government of a free creature.* What glory is there in the government of a slave? or of what is less than even a slave, in point of freedom, a "*machine?*" We can form no conception of wisdom which equals

that displayed in the government of a creature whose obedience is love; hence the very highest degree of that wisdom is seen in the government of a perfectly free will. The more perfectly and absolutely free the will is, originating purely of itself the acts of the mind, the more glorious is that wisdom by which all these acts are regulated, and led along the path of honor and of holiness. The idea that " the history of this world, in all things, great and small, is just the history of events preordained of God from eternity "—every thing *fixed*, *determined*, and *irrevocable*, because of Almighty power to carry out these determinations—where is wisdom required to govern the procedure which is all so determined? On the other hand, admit the perfect freedom of man's will,—that every one of his voluntary actions originates with himself, and then conceive of the wisdom displayed in controlling even the unholy wrath which is contrary to every desire and design of God—the fruit of man's free and wicked choice—so that it shall accomplish the purposes of his goodness and mercy, and we have before us that by which some conception of unsearchable wisdom may be formed. Sin is thus seen as a strange and unnatural intrusion upon the wisely created, and wisely governed universe of God—a creation of the will which He has formed in freedom—an abomination contrary to every desire and design of His infinite mind of purity and love; and yet, though strange and foreign to His every desire and design, not beyond the provisions of a government so wisely framed as to meet every possible or conceivable exigency. This is the true character of the government of God. The idea of His ordaining sin that He might overrule it, is wretched. It is like a king being represented as creating an enemy that he might conquer him, and taking good care that he should not be such an enemy as would either be able to cope with his power, or overreach his skill! In an earthly king the idea would be beneath contempt—how infinitely more so in the great Jehovah.

But in carrying out this truth of God's wisdom being glorified in the freedom of the will of man, we must not overlook the fact, that it is the freedom of will that emphatically gives God the title of "KING of *kings*." If every action is *fixed*, and that from eternity, how can these be the actions of "kings?" Where is the honor of being king of such kings? But if no action is fixed, if the spirit is created and maintained in perfect freedom—free to originate its own volitions—then is the King of immortals the King of kings indeed; and when He so rules as to secure their obedience, it is the obedience of kings that He receives. This is the wisdom of God.

3. *The wisdom of God is illustrated in His* REDEMPTION *of free creatures*. The idea of an *irresistible* influence or power, exercised by God over the mind of man, is ever associated with that of universal predestination. By these the whole glory of the wisdom of God, in His plan for the recovery of lost souls, is hid in inexplicable mystery. He is made to appear constructing a vast and incalculably costly system of motive, and at the same time we are told that "motive" is nothing—that it is a se-

cret, irresistible power, by which alone the will is turned, and that every act calling for a ransom, as well as every act of the soul that is ransomed, was *fixed* from all eternity. There is an entire absence of all consistency between the doctrine that all was irrevocably fixed, and the doctrine that God required to make the infinitely costly sacrifice of His dearest object, in order that men might be saved from that sin which He Himself had foreordained! This inconsistency at once disappears when you admit that sin is the intrusion—the wicked and unprovoked intrusion—of a free and rebelling creature on the plans and creations of a holy God. And when we see that God so loved man that He would neither destroy him nor annihilate his freedom, but that, to save both, He provided the incomprehensibly costly sacrifice of the cross, then we have the field of redemption opened to us for the adoration of Divine Wisdom. Sin is the enemy of God and the curse of man—a stranger in the universe, yet not such but that all its dreadful power is met in the work of Jesus. In that work, the language of God is most strikingly verified—" I drew thee with the bands of a man—with the cords of love;" and the same is true of the whole work of the Holy Spirit, as that work is described in the Bible. The creature, even in the utmost state of depravity, is ever brought before the mind as perfectly free, and yet as drawn by mighty motives to the heart of God from the deepest depths of misery and guilt. O! my hearer, it is well worth your most careful effort to study the unsearchable wisdom of God in meeting the enormous difficulty introduced by sin;

and when you have expended somewhat of adequate attention on the subject, you will be constrained to wonder at the *depths* of God's wisdom in a very different way from that in which those do who look at inexplicable inconsistencies, and because they can neither vindicate nor reconcile them, are led to exclaim, "Oh, the depths!"

That is not necessarily *deep* of which we can not see the bottom. It may be only *muddy*, and it will not cost great effort to see that all the *depth* that exists in the doctrine of universal predestination is simply in the impossibility of seeing any clear truth in it. The idea has been too long taken for granted by men, that that must needs be unfathomable which defies the efforts of the mind to understand it. They have long been accustomed to come from hearing a sermon which they could not see through, with the exclamation upon their lips, "That was a *deep* sermon!" The time is more than come, we trust, when such ideas of depth shall cease to find a place in the minds of men. When sailing upon the calm, clear, transparent bosom of the mighty ocean, what is it that impresses you with the idea of its depth? Is it not the fact that your eye penetrates, without difficulty, many fathoms down, while you *see* that there are fathoms still beyond the depth to which the eye has reached? It is the very *clearness* that gives the true conception of the depth. So is it with the wisdom of God in reality. There is no need of crying, "Oh, the depth!" in regard to that wisdom, simply because it is impossible to reconcile its acts and purposes. The depth is seen in the clearness with which they can be reconciled, and yet in the greatness of their mighty comprehension, as they compass eternity itself and open the bosom of a righteous God to the eternal confidence of guilty men.

In concluding this lecture, let me press again upon the mind of my hearer the high privilege, and most sacred duty, that arise to us out of the reality of our freedom. Is it not a privilege to serve Him who loved us, and gave Himself for us, with *spontaneous* service? Is it not a privilege, knowing that we are as free as God Himself can make us, freely, and conscious of our liberty, to adore the wisdom of our Father, and to yield ourselves fully, constantly, and for ever, to the directions of that matchless wisdom? Is it not a high privilege to enjoy, and most freely to exercise that confidence which this matchless wisdom is fitted to inspire? But as is our privilege so is our duty. Oh, my fellow-immortal! let us realize our responsibility in being created and placed in the position of *free* creatures. No one can realize this without also realizing the necessity—the blessed necessity—that is laid upon us to yield ourselves fully to our God, or to incur the most *incalculable* amount of guilt and condemnation. What shall we answer at last when our *freedom*, and our *responsibility* and *obligations*, are brought fully before us, if we have disregarded them all? How shall we be able to look at that sacrifice which God has made to ransom us, and at that work of the Holy Spirit by which He has sought to win us to a *free*, spontaneous choice of His love, if we have "always resisted" His infinitely wise and most gracious work? Oh, now is the time to realize our danger! and also to realize our duty, and with all the power of will with which He has endowed us, to be for ever devoted to Him! Let us adore Him who has made us kings. Let Him have that consecration, and that allegiance, of which only the King of kings is worthy. Oh, let Him have the everlasting song of our ransomed souls in acknowledgment of His wisdom in our creation, in our government, and, above all, in our ransom and deliverance!

LECTURE III.

PREDESTINATION AND THE JUSTICE OF GOD.

There is nothing of greater importance to man than just views of the moral character of his God. If he has false conceptions of this, his own moral character, and all that depends on it, will bear the taint of the falsehood. Not only so, but the closer in such a case that his mind is brought into fellowship with his God, the more will this error become an attribute of his own moral nature.* In this lecture, therefore, I shall aim to present to the mind right views of the JUSTICE of Jehovah, as well as to remove the false views that are given of it by the doctrine of universal predestination.

I. LET US CONSIDER SOME OF THE LEADING FEATURES OF THE JUSTICE OF GOD AS REVEALED IN THE BIBLE.

Under this head, I shall endeavor to state clearly both the general principles of divine justice, and those more particularly bearing upon the subject in hand.

1. *The attribute of Justice in God is that* DISPOSITION *of His moral nature which infallibly leads Him* TO DO THAT WHICH IS RIGHT. This is universally acknowledged to be Justice. He who

---

* See the Philosophy of the Plan of Salvation, chap. i.

is disposed with all his heart to do that which is right, is a just being. The question by which His justice is most emphatically declared is this—" Shall not the Judge of all the earth DO RIGHT?" Every sane and reflecting mind is compelled to answer this question in the affirmative. There is difference of opinion as to what IS RIGHT, but there can be none as to the certainty of the justice of God.

2. *This attribute of Justice in God supposes the existence of* A PRINCIPLE OF RIGHT. It stands upon the granted truth, that certain actions, or courses of action, *are right*. This is a most important truth connected with the doctrine of the justice of God. The question, "Shall not the Judge of all the earth DO RIGHT?" not only supposes that there is right as distinguished from wrong, but also that right and wrong are not such hidden principles as to be secrets to men. The greatest possible doom is pronounced against those who confound these all-important principles:—" Woe to them that call evil good, and good evil; that put darkness for light, and light for darkness; that put bitter for sweet, and sweet for bitter." (Is. v. 20.) It must be regarded, then, as a Bible and fixed truth, that there is a principle of right which men are bound to understand and pursue.

3. *This principle of right* IS ONE AND THE SAME *in all possible actions, or courses of action*. This is a most inestimable truth, and one which seems to be forgotten, if not denied, by those who defend the doctrine of universal predestination. It is, however, invincible reality. Just as the principle of truth is the same in God that it is in man, so is

the principle of right the same in both. That which is false in man can not be true in God; and that which is in itself wrong in man can not be right in God. Mark, I do not hold that every particular action that would be wrong in man, must, therefore, be wrong in God. This would be absurd; but that every action, or course of action, the principle of which *is wrong*, must be equally wrong to all. If the *principle* of the action be wrong in man it must also be wrong in God.

In order to verify this, we have only to remember that we have the following command—" Be ye therefore followers of God as dear children." (Eph. v. 1.) Now, if this command mean any thing, it must at least mean this, that the principles which we see to be those of the conduct of God must be those of our conduct. We are not called upon to follow Him in the exercise of omnipotence, but, with the power we have, to follow Him so far as we can, proceeding exactly in our sphere as He does in His. This all-important truth is still farther verified by the fact, that God reasons with man as to the justice of His own dealings. We shall turn attention to this more fully afterward. At present it is only necessary to remind the hearer of the fact, that God, in the fifth chapter of Isaiah, commands the men of Judah to *judge* between Himself and them. This fact, which runs through the whole Bible, is fatal—infallibly fatal—to that mode of defense which is used for the doctrine of eternal reprobation. As a specimen of this, I quote the following: —" How exceedingly presumptuous it is only to inquire into the causes of the divine will; which is, in fact, and is justly entitled to be, the cause of every thing that exists."* Compare this charge of presumption with the command of God to the men of Judah. "JUDGE YE," says Jehovah. "It is presumptuous even to inquire," says human authority. Let us rejoice that the haughty air of the tyrant, whose course of action must not be canvassed, is infinitely removed from the dignity of our God. He makes His ways plain in every case where the full and *intelligent* satisfaction of the conscience of man is concerned—so plain, that even His enemies may be judges of their own cause. This is indubitable evidence that *right* is one and the same in God and in man—that if the principle of an action be wrong for man, it is wrong, and, therefore, impossible with God.

4. *It follows clearly from what has now been stated, that God can not condemn in man that principle of conduct which He pursues Himself.* This is declared to be criminal in the highest degree in the creature. Paul says, in his epistle to the Romans, "And thinkest thou this, O man, that judgest them that do such things, and doest the same, that thou shalt escape the righteous judgment of God?" (Ch. ii. 3.) This is a most emphatic declaration, that the principle of condemning in others that which we practice ourselves, is criminal, and certain to be punished. This is a most self-evident, but most important principle of justice. It leads us to the conclusion, that that which God condemns in man He never will do Himself. If this principle is denied, then there is an end to all confidence in

* Calvin's Institutes, book iii. ch. xxii. sec. 2.

the character of God. If He may do Himself that which in the very spirit and essence of it He condemns and punishes in man, there is, and there must be, an end to confidence in the justice of God. There is an end to all understanding of right and wrong as eternal and immutable principles of action. Such a consequence wrapt up in any doctrine is sufficient for its destruction.

II. LET US NOW CONSIDER THE APPLICATION OF THESE PRINCIPLES TO UNIVERSAL PREDESTINATION.

We shall endeavor to take that doctrine in the words of its own highest advocates, and as it bears upon the truth of the justice of God.

1. *God condemns the principle of doing evil that good may come.* The mind of Paul most emphatically, and with abhorrence, renounces this principle. His words to the Romans are these—"And not rather (as we be slanderously reported, and as some affirm that we say) let us do evil that good may come, whose damnation is just." Mark carefully, my hearer, the *strength* of the condemnation which the inspired apostle declared against the principle of doing evil that good may come. Now, this is the *fundamental* principle of the whole doctrine of reprobation, without which the doctrine of *universal* predestination perishes. It is impossible to deny that this is the foundation of the doctrine, if you read it in the words of those who hold it. Let us see it as thus stated by those who should be able to state it aright. I quote again from the book that claims attention as the confession of

thousands on thousands of the professing Christians of Scotland :—" By the decree of God, FOR THE MANIFESTATION OF HIS GLORY, some men and angels are predestinated unto everlasting life, and others foreordained to everlasting death. These angels and men, thus predestinated and foreordained, are particularly and unchangeably designed, and their number is so certain and definite, that it can not be either increased or diminished." * The fundamental principle of this passage is, that in order to promote the good of His own glory, God decreed unchangeably the eternal destruction of men. I quote, however, still further the statements of this doctrine, to show that this decree of condemnation was not passed because of *sin being foreseen* in those to be condemned :—" Although God knows whatsoever may or can come to pass upon all supposed conditions, yet hath He not decreed anything because He foresaw it future, or as that which would come to pass upon such conditions." * Such is the solemn declaration regarding God made by the vast majority of professing Christians in this land. But we must quote further. Lest it should be supposed that God, from eternity, decreed thus the damnation of some men for His glory, but left them to secure it, or cause it of their own free will, the following statement is made in regard to the reprobate :—" Those, therefore, whom He has created to a life of shame and a death of destruction, that they might be instruments of His wrath, and examples of His severity, HE CAUSES to reach their appointed end, sometimes depriving them of an op-

---

* Confession of Faith, chap. iii.

portunity of hearing the Word, sometimes by the preaching of it increases their blindness and stupidity." Again,—"The supreme Lord, therefore, by depriving of the communication of His light, and leaving in darkness, those whom He hath reprobated, makes way for the accomplishment of His predestination." And again,—"I know that it appears harsh to some when faith is attributed to the reprobate; since Paul affirms it to be the fruit of election. But this difficulty is easily solved: for though none are illuminated to faith, or truly feel the efficacy of the gospel, but such as are foreordained to salvation, yet experience shows that the reprobate are sometimes affected with emotions very similar to those of the elect, so that, in their opinion, they in no respect differ from the elect. Wherefore it is not at all absurd that a taste of heavenly gifts is abscribed to them by the apostle, and a temporary faith in Christ; not that they truly perceive the energy of spiritual grace and clear light of faith, but because the Lord, to render their guilt more manifest and inexcusable, insinuates Himself into their minds as far as His goodness can be enjoyed without the spirit of adoption." The whole of these statements proceed upon the idea that God has not only determined the destiny of the reprobate, but that He takes care so to arrange every thing concerning them, as that His decree of their destruction shall not be counteracted. Lest it should be supposed that God only *permits* men to fulfill His secret decree, and that their sin, though permitted, is contrary to their real will, it is said further,—"It is not probable, however, that man procured his own destruction by the mere permission, and without any appointment of God. As though God had not determined what He would choose to be the condition of the principal of His creatures. I shall not hesitate, therefore, to confess with Augustine, 'that the will of God is the necessity of things, and what He has willed will necessarily come to pass.'"* If it is possible to express the idea that God has decreed, and that He does actually accomplish the blinding and ruin of the reprobate that His own glory (!) may be promoted, it is taught by these statements of the great apostle of predestination, and by the Scottish confession itself. We can not see the possibility of holding the doctrine on any other ground that will give even a shadow of plausibility to it. It is plausible to hold to the great importance of the honor of God—and the pretense that the ascription of reprobation to Him honors Him, makes this horrid libel on His character pass with many; but it is impossible to make it out less than His decreeing evil that good may come, and the idea that God will do that, which even Paul renounces with abhorrence, should surely be sufficient to stamp with eternal infamy the doctrine that is founded upon such an idea. Oh, my hearer! think not that you have such a God as this represents Him to be. No!—"A God of truth and without iniquity—just and right is He." Hence, the doctrine of His foreordaining whatsoever comes to pass must be rejected as a most fearful error.

2. *The doctrine of universal predestination involves the idea that God condemns and eternally*

* Calvin's Inst., book iii. chap. xxiv.

punishes that which He Himself decreed and determines to be. It is impossible to conceive of injustice if this be not the most fearful principle that can bear that name. This doctrine not only holds that man is condemned for that which he could not possibly avoid, as he could not possibly defeat the determination of Omnipotence, but that man is condemned for doing that very thing which God willed to be done. The difficulty with some of my hearers will be to believe that any human being can hold such a doctrine. In addition, therefore, to that which I have already quoted, stating and illustrating that God has " foreordained whatsoever comes to pass," I quote further. The argument is *stated*, and, according to predestination, *answered*, in the following passage :—" ' Why should God impute to the fault of man those things which were rendered necessary by His predestination? What should they do? Should they resist His decrees? This would be vain, for it would be impossible. Therefore, they are not punished for those things of which God's predestination is the principal cause.' Here I shall refrain from the defense commonly resorted to by ecclesiastical writers, that the foreknowedge of God prevents not man from being considered as a sinner, since God foresees man's evils, not His own. For then the cavil would not stop here; it would rather be urged, that still God might, if He would, have provided against the evil He foresaw, and not having done this, He created man expressly to this end, that he might so conduct himself in the world: 'but if, by the Divine providence, man was created in such a state as afterward to do whatever he actually does, he ought not to be charged with guilt for things which he can not avoid, and to which the will of God constrains him.' Let us see how this difficulty should be solved. In the first place, the declaration of Solomon ought to be universally admitted, that 'the Lord hath made all things for Himself; yea, even the wicked for the day of evil.' Observe, all things being at God's disposal, and the decision of salvation or death belonging to Him, He orders all things by His counsel and decrees in such a manner, that some men are born devoted from the womb to certain death, that His name may be glorified in their destruction. If any one pleads that no necessity was imposed on them by the providence of God, but rather that they were created by Him in such a state, in consequence of His foresight of their future depravity, it will amount to nothing. The old writers used, indeed, to adopt this solution, though not without some degree of hesitation; but the schoolmen satisfy themselves with it, as though it admitted of no opposition. I will readily grant, indeed, that mere foreknowledge lays no necessity on the creatures, though this is not universally admitted; for there are some who maintain it to be the actual cause of what comes to pass. But Valla, a man otherwise not much versed in theology, appears to me to have discovered superior acuteness and judiciousness, by showing that this controversy is unnecessary, because both life and death are acts of God's will, rather than of His foreknowledge. If God simply foresaw the fates of men, and did not also dispose and fix them by His determination, there would be room to agitate the question, whether His providence or foresight rendered them at all necessary; but since He foresees future events only in consequence of His decree that they shall happen, it is useless to contend about foreknowledge, while it is evident that all things come to pass rather by ordination and decree."*

It is impossible to soften the meaning of this passage so as to make it even seem to mean less than it says. It is itself rather an argument against all attempt to soften the doctrines of its author;—it is condemnation to those who would apologize for the strength and fearful harshness of his views. He seeks to render it out of the question to inquire whether God's providence and foresight rendered all events *necessary*. It is to be received as a doctrine not at all admitting of question, that all is *inevitably fixed*. Calvin had too much love for the doctrine of predestination to be afraid of speaking out upon it in most unambiguous terms. But observe the defense he makes for the doctrine. Look for the arguments that are to rise and confute the "profane complaint" which, he says, is made against his theory. He does excite the expectation of *proof* in the commencement of the section before us. He has asserted that God not only decreed, but also brought to pass all the events (including the sins of men) that take place in the universe; and this is doubted,—a powerful and most obvious objection is started, and he seems to prepare himself for the full removal of the objection. How does he proceed? Does he attempt to *show the*

* Calvin's Institutes.

evidence in the case? No. It will be seen that the defense of the doctrine which I now seek to oppose, as contained in the passage above quoted, is simply a redoubled assertion of its verity. There is no other defense attempted by him who is supposed to be the very greatest of the advocates of the doctrine. Calvin and Augustine unite to say, regarding the demanded defense of their doctrine—"*faithful ignorance is better than presumptuous knowledge!*" and that is the SUM of their answer to the objection which is now stated. Let us see if this answer betters the case. It is said that God not only decreed, but actually secures the carrying out of His decrees in the sin and condemnation of men. We say—to hold such a doctrine *is to ascribe injustice to God*. Our objection is a FATAL one to the doctrine. What does their answer to that objection prove? Simply that they have no real reply with which to meet the objection. It comes up before them in the light of a clear statement, and all that they do is, to escape into the darkness of pretended mystery. This is the most feeble of all possible defenses, and sadly unworthy of the great minds that used it. Is there any depth of mystery in ascribing to God the condemnation and punishment of that which He Himself *decrees and brings about?* If there be a depth, it is that of the most unaccountable folly and sin. O! my hearer, are you prepared to hold by the doctrine before us? Are you prepared to believe that your just God will pursue such a course as that now represented? He so loved justice, and the manifestation of it too, that He would not propose the pardon of injustice on a lower ground than the sacrifice of Calvary. Are you capable of believing that He will perpetrate that which He has condemned in the death and agonies of His beloved Son? Are you not rather glad to escape from the miserable delusions of men *called* great, to the plain declarations of the Word of God. "As I live, saith the Lord God, I have no pleasure in the death of the wicked." No: their death, instead of being the result of His decree, is contrary to every feeling of His heart, and every principle of His nature. It is the creation of their own free determination to continue in sin. Perish, then, forever, that most odious of falsehoods, that "God foreordained whatsoever comes to pass."

3. *The doctrine with which we have now to do, involves the idea that God is a "respecter of persons."* It is evident that those who plead for the doctrine totally fail to repel this objection, as they more than fail to repel those that I have already stated. The idea is, that in the multitude of angels and men seen by the Divine Omniscience from all eternity, God made this distinction—that He decreed the one part to holiness and happiness, the other to sin and death; and *we are not* to seek the cause of this decree in any foreseen difference in the creatures, but to find it in the *will* of the Creator. Now, what is "respect of persons?" Is it the preference of a Jew to a Gentile? Manifestly not. A Jew might be preferred to a Gentile on a sound principle of right and benevolence. Is it the preference of a rich man to a poor man? No; for this preference may be entertained and no sound

principle infringed. Is it, then, the preference of a master to a servant? No; for a master may be preferred, in certain cases, to a servant, on sound enough principles. What, then, is respect of persons? It may be answered: "It is preferring a Jew *merely* because he is a Jew,—a rich man merely because he is rich,—and a master merely because he is a master." But the question still returns: How is this wrong? I answer—because the reason of preference is not sufficient to justify it. This is the root of the error. A preference of one man to another must have a *reason*, and a sufficient reason, on which to stand. If the reasons for a preference are not sufficient, then the preference of one man to another is respect of persons; if so, what are we to make of the doctrine that God prefers one man to another *for no reason at all*,—that He so far prefers the one to the other, that He decrees the one to hell and the other to heaven, while His decree is not to be *supposed* to rest upon the difference between the one man and the other? This is the crime of respect of persons ascribed to God in an infinite degree. The man that is not made to feel his soul aroused within him against such an infamous calumny of Jehovah, has surely little regard for his God. Mark, then, the miserable nature of this attempt that is made to alter the force of the glorious Scripture declaration, that God is no respecter of persons. It is an attempt to substitute the shadow for the substance, or a *few* of the practical bearings of a principle for the principle itself. Search into the truth on this part of our subject, and you will find that the deeper the search the more clear will be your conviction, that the sin of being a respecter of persons is the sin of preferring one man to another, without any reason of a sufficient character in the object of your preference. This is respecting the *person*, regardless of the reasons of the case. The very *words* of the Book of God on the point show this to be the sin; and were God to accept a man altogether irrespective of the reasons found in the man's case, and to prefer that man to another who is in exactly the same position, He would do that which, in the very essence and letter of the thing done, would be the acceptance of a *person*—it would be preferring the *person*, and not the truth and righteousness in the case; it would be a sacrifice of all just principle on the part of God. O! let us rejoice that our God "is no respecter of persons;" let us glory in the Bible, by which we are enabled, on His own authority, to make such a declaration. Let us devote our best energies to the everlasting and total banishment of those falsehoods that have so long triumphed over the prostrate souls of men, and led them to think of a Sovereign God as a respecter of persons.

It is unnecessary to proceed farther with the proof of the truth I have sought to establish. We have seen that the doctrine of universal predestination involves that God does evil that good may come,—that it involves the idea that God condemns others for that which He Himself decrees and carries out,—and that it holds Him forth to man as chargeable with the injustice of respect of persons in an infinite degree. It will not do for the advocates of the doctrine to grow big with indignation at these assertions: let them *disprove* them. It is vain for such to put their theory in the throne of Jehovah, and then ask, " Who art thou that repliest against God?" Let them first prove that their doctrine is of God. It is also vain to speak of *mystery*, when the only thing involved in the mystery is the question how they are to prove their assertions. Let them bring their proof out of the impenetrable gloom in which it abides, and then they may be permitted to speak of mysteries. But, O! my hearer, be it yours to rejoice that you have a God of unspotted and unyielding justice, whose love is free to you, through the honorable propitiation of that justice in the atonement of Jesus. Let your soul be for ever relieved from the plague of universal predestination; see that it is but a dream of the night—a phantom created by ignorance, and destined to vanish with the approach of light. Be freed from its mystifying and perplexing snares, by regarding it, in its true character, as a falsehood, and realizing the solemnity and responsibility of the position which you occupy as a free subject of a righteous God, enjoying that blessed confidence which a clear and intelligent sense of His infallible rectitude is fitted to inspire. You are free to form the strongest conceptions of His justice, for that is not now your enemy, but your friend. Jesus has answered for your guilt; and the infinitely righteous Jehovah invites you to repose in His mercy and love, and to be as really His child as if you had not sinned. How glorifying to God whose Spirit has ever abhorred iniquity, to see Him, after making atonement to justice for your sin, declaring His infinite desire that you should enjoy His eternal friendship. O! my hearer, be not satisfied with *merely* renouncing the doctrine of predestination, but gladly embrace the love of your propitious God. "Acquaint yourself now with Him, and be at peace."

LECTURE IV.

PREDESTINATION AND THE TRUTH OF GOD.

No subject, connected with the character of God, can exceed in importance the truthfulness of that character. If this is rendered obscure, or has a suspicion cast upon it, the soul of man in vain seeks for a resting-place. The doctrine that may be rightly charged with even the *concealment* of this attribute of God, is worthy of the most unequivocal renunciation by every immortal being. We shall see, in the course of our inquiry, that the doctrine of universal predestination not only conceals, and renders doubtful, the divine veracity and honesty, but that it is impossible to reconcile the doctrine with the belief in that veracity at all. In pursuing this subject, I shall first state some of the more manifest principles of truthfulness, and then apply these to the doctrine in hand, in connection with some of the dealings of Jehovah with men.

I. LET US CONSIDER SOME OF THE MORE PROMINENT FEATURES OF TRUTHFUL CONDUCT.

The declaration of Scripture, confirmed in the conscience of every man, is, that Jehovah is "A GOD OF TRUTH." We can only truly value this blessed testimony in proportion as we see and value the real nature of truth itself.

1. *To use words the obvious sense of which is false, is contrary to a character of veracity.* To utter words that convey to the mind of another a false idea when that person takes the words in their common and obvious import, is to utter falsehood. To do this is infinitely inconsistent with the character of a truthful God. Yet we shall see that were the doctrine of predestination true, as we have seen it stated in the words of its advocates, there are many of the declarations of God that, in the obvious and common meaning of the words, as well as from the connection in which these words occur, would convey falsehood to the mind. We shall see that were this doctrine true, there are most solemn declarations of God that would be plainly and palpably untrue. Now, plain, unambiguous falsehood is the most palpable proof we can have of the absence of truthfulness in those who make the false statement.

2. *But if one speak so as to make that* SEEM TRUE *which is not really so, his conduct is inconsistent with truthfulness.* I mean, in this remark, to point out the course that may be pursued by a person who does not make statements that in themselves are untrue, but who utters statements that *imply* other statements of a false kind. For example, if a man makes a statement to me that he invites me to a feast—it is quite true that he invites me, but the fact of this invitation implies that he has a feast provided for me, and that it is his *real* desire that I should accept the invitation. If he has no feast for me, and does not really *intend* that I should accept the invitation, the utterance of that

invitation is itself an act of base falsehood. Or if a man professes to pity me when I am ill, and actually sheds tears over me in token of pity, this *implies* that he is really desiring, and will do his utmost for my recovery. If he has an infallible remedy in his possession, and is withholding it at the very moment that he is weeping over my illness, his conduct is false, and will be denounced as such by the universe of mind.

3. *Although involved in the former, I may mention particularly, that speaking with a mental reservation is universally contrary to the attribute of truth.* If you speak to a man so that an impression is made on his mind which would be completely destroyed were you to utter all you know, you are not speaking according to truth. This blessed and divine attribute courts the light. It has no secrets that contradict that which is uttered, and whenever such secrets are kept, the Spirit of Truth is not there. Now, we shall see speedily, that it is impossible to show any one of these features in the conduct of God, if the doctrine of universal predestination be true. In other words, it will be seen that this doctrine, if admitted, destroys the idea of truth in God.

II. LET US CONSIDER SOME OF THE PROMINENT ACTS AND DECLARATIONS OF GOD IN THE LIGHT OF THESE PRINCIPLES, AND ALSO IN THAT. OF THE DOCTRINE IN QUESTION.

Observe, my hearer, that truth, and he who has truth on his side, never seeks refuge in darkness;

and as I apply these principles, and the acts and declarations of God, to the doctrine especially of God's foreordination of sin and death, it can not be tolerated in the man who opposes on the pretense of being the advocate of truth that he should plead unfathomable mystery.

1. *Consider the conduct of God in connection with the fall of man.* The doctrine I oppose is, that this fatal crime was fixed to be by God from all eternity. This doctrine is stated as follows:—"I confess indeed that all the decendants of Adam fell by the divine will into that miserable condition in which they are now involved; and this is what I asserted from the beginning, that we must always return at last to the sovereign determination of God's will, the cause of which is hidden in himself." * Again,—"It is an awful decree, I confess; but no one can deny that God foreknew the future final state of man before He created him, and that He did foreknow it, because it was appointed by His own decree." Again,—"For the first man fell because the Lord had determined it should so happen." There is no ambiguity in these statements. If words have meaning they declare the fall, or first sin of man, to be the result of God's irrevocable and impassable decree. Now, I affirm, and will immediately prove, that if these statements are admitted, it is *impossible* to make it appear that God adheres to the truth. Hear what He says to our first parents, in reference to the act of disobedience now under consideration:—"The tree of knowledge of good and evil, which is in the midst of the garden,

* Calvin's Institutes, book iii. ch. xxiii.

ye shall not eat of it, for in the day that thou eatest thereof THOU SHALT SURELY DIE." Now, what *appears* from this command and most dreadful threatening of instant death? Does it not *appear* that it is God's determination that, if possible, they shall be prevented from falling? Place yourselves in their situation, and try to conceive of what your impression would have been from the words of God. Would you have gathered from these words the idea, that He had *secretly determined* that the very crime which He had threatened with death should be committed nevertheless? Look at the inexpressibly awful calumny that is made to rest upon God by the fearful doctrine of a predestinated fall. Is it not high time that we had awakened out of sleep, and had come to the help of the Lord against the mighty? The charge against God of decreeing the fall, and at the same time threatening death if His decree was fulfilled, is surely sufficient to shake the confidence of any man in that system that involves such a monstrous absurdity. Oh! my hearer! beware of indifference on such a point as this. If you are jealous of your own good name, much more may you be so of God's.

2. *Consider the conduct of God immediately after the fall of man.* Let us ask if that conduct is such as accords with the idea that the fall was the fulfillment of His own decree? Was this what appeared from His words to our first parents and to the tempter? Read His words:—" And the Lord said unto the serpent, Because thou hast done this, thou art cursed above all cattle, and above every beast of the field: upon thy belly shalt thou go,

and dust shalt thou eat all the days of thy life. And I will put enmity between thee and the woman, and between thy seed and her seed; it shall bruise thy head, and thou shalt bruise his heel. Unto the woman He said, I will greatly multiply thy sorrow and thy conception: in sorrow thou shalt bring forth children; and thy desire shall be to thy husband and he shall rule over thee. And unto Adam He said, Because thou hast hearkened unto the voice of thy wife, and hast eaten of the tree, of which I commanded thee saying, Thou shalt not eat of it; cursed is the ground for thy sake; in sorrow shalt thou eat of it all the days of thy life: thorns also and thistles shall it bring forth to thee; and thou shalt eat the herb of the field. In the sweat of thy face shalt thou eat bread, till thou return unto the ground: for out of it wast thou taken: for dust thou art, and unto dust shalt thou return." Gen. iii. 14–19.

Now, my hearer, think on these words of God, and ask, Are they fitted to make an impression in accordance with the statement that Satan and man had just accomplished the fulfillment of that decree which Jehovah had fixed, and that they had produced the very thing which He had ordained to take place, in order that He might honor Himself thereby? It can not be that your preceptions of truth are so blind and perverted, as that you shall fail to see that, if the decree in question be true, God did not act so as to make the truth appear, but so as to make an impression contrary to that truth. I call upon you, in the name of that God who is thus calumniated by those who profess to do Him honor, not only to renounce the vile falsehood of universal predestination for yourself, but to be stirred up to seek its everlasting extinction from the minds of men.

3. *Consider the promise of a Saviour made by God at the fall.* This is made in the pronouncing of the curse on the serpent in these words,—" He shall bruise thy head." We have the full statement of the meaning of this promise in the Epistle to the Hebrews (ch. ii. 14–15), " Forasmuch, then, as the children are partakers of flesh and blood, He also Himself likewise took part of the same, that through death He might destroy him that had the power of death, that is, the devil; and deliver them who, through fear of death, were all their lifetime subject to bondage." Let my hearer ask his own mind what is made to appear in all this. Is it that the devil had just done that which God had pleased should be done, and which He had from all eternity decreed to take place? Again, does it accord with the idea that the great Saviour was to die in order to atone for a fulfillment of Jehovah's decree? I confess, my hearer, that I blush for humanity in asking such questions as these; yet I am forced to ask them. Thousands upon thousands of the inhabitants of Scotland, if asked, " What are the decrees of God?" tell you that they " are His eternal purpose, according to the counsel of His will, whereby, for His own glory, He hath foreordained whatsoever comes to pass." Ay, thousands are prepared to tell you of the most disgraceful acts of their lives, " that was before us and we could not get past it." The vast majority of Scotland's profess-

ing Christians are solemnly bound to that doctrine as the standard of their religion and the confession of their faith. We are thus *compelled* to ask such questions, and to press them upon the attention of men. Does it then *appear*, from the promised sacrifice of Jesus, that that sacrifice was an atonement for that which God Himself had determined should be done? If this is to be held, there is an end to all understanding of truth, as that by which the reality and not the falsehood is made apparent.

4. *Consider the bearing of this doctrine upon the gospel as more fully proclaimed.* The more clearly we hear the glad tidings of salvation, the more striking is the contradiction manifest between it and the doctrine now before us. That doctrine involves what is stated in the following words:— "In regard, again, to the other light in which Christ's purchase may be viewed as a purchase, not of certain benefits for men but of men themselves, there is room for an important distinction. In right of His merit, His service, and His sacrifice, all are given into His hands, and all are His. All, therefore, may be said to be bought by Him, inasmuch as by His humiliation, obedience, and death, He has obtained, as by purchase, a right over all—He has got all under His power. But it is for very different purposes and ends. The reprobate are His to be judged; the elect are His to be saved. As to the former, it is no ransom or redemption, fairly so called. He has won them—bought them, if you will—but it is that He may so dispose of them as to glorify the retributive righteousness of God in their condemnation—aggravated as that condemnation

must be by their rejection of Himself. This is no propitiation in any sense at all—no offering of Himself to bear their sins—no bringing in of a perfect righteousness on their account; but an office or function which He has obtained for Himself by the same work—or has intrusted to Him for the sake of the same shedding of blood—by which He expiated the sins of His people, as their true and proper substitute, and merited their salvation, as their representative and head—an office or function, moreover, which He undertakes solely in His people's behalf, and which He executes faithfully for their good, as well as for His Father's glory."* - Mark well this extraordinary passage; and let us prepare to contrast it with the truth as it is in Jesus. Here you have a very bold and most confident assertion that the death of Jesus is "NO RANSOM" for a large portion of mankind. It is something in virtue of which He has got them into His hands to destroy them, but it is no propitiation for them. This is said to be the truth according to the doctrine of universal predestination. No statements can be more distinct and unequivocal, showing that Jesus DID NOT bear the sins of the reprobate, so as to furnish them with good news, from the fact of His death and resurrection. Let us, then, turn to the declarations of God, which are said to be His *revealed will*, and see how they agree with this which is said to be the secret reality. He says of Jesus by His inspired forerunner,—" Behold the Lamb of God bearing the sin of the world!" I quote literally from the original of John i. 29. Again, "There is one God

* Candlish on the Atonement, pp. 7 and 8.

and one Mediator between God and man, the man Christ Jesus, who gave Himself a ransom for all." Again,—" He is the propitiation for our sins, and not for ours only, but also for the sins of the whole world." This is the gospel, for Paul says so in addressing the Corinthians (1 Cor. xv.). He declares the gospel to be, that Christ died for our sins, and was buried and rose again. Now, hear Jesus, " Go into all the world, and preach the gospel to every creature." How does this accord with what I have quoted above? What is the impression which this language is fitted to make? Is it not this—that Jesus bore the sins of " every creature " to whom the *good news* of His death is sent? Is not this the meaning of the commission—the meaning that lies on the very *surface* of it—that meaning which every simple mind, on hearing it, would receive as the intention of the speakers or writers of the words? Are we to believe that, in giving the commission of the gospel that it might be carried to every creature, Jesus had this mental reservation—that the great majority of those to whom this gospel was sent were by Himself decreed to everlasting death, and entirely excluded from all benefit in His great propitiation by that irrevocable decree? No wonder that men tell us that they are incapable of reconciling these things. But it is matter of wonder that any man in his senses should state that which, if admitted to be true, entirely destroys the very idea of God being a God of truth.

5. *Consider the appeal of God, which He makes on oath, by the prophet Ezekiel.* Think of the impression which these words are fitted to make : " As

I live, saith the Lord, I have NO PLEASURE in the death of the wicked." Take this most solemn and awful disclaimer, and put it side by side with the following doctrine :—" Whom God passes by, therefore, He reprobates, and from *no other cause* than His determination to exclude them from the inheritance which He predestinates for His children."*
Again,—" The rest of mankind (that is the reprobate) God WAS PLEASED, according to the unsearchable counsel of His own will, whereby He extendeth or withholdeth mercy as HE PLEASETH, for the glory of His sovereign power over His creatures, to pass by, and to ordain them to dishonor and wrath for their sins, to the praise of His glorious justice." † Which of these two representations of God's mind are we to adopt ? If we take the first as really presenting the truth, we can not take the second. The first is God's declaration *on oath*, that He has NO pleasure in the death of the wicked ; the second is man's declaration that God has pleasure in that death, and sternly forbids us to seek the *first cause* of that death anywhere but in the will of God ! If the second be true, the first is a profession irreconcilable with the truth ; and hence we must either renounce it, or give up truth as an attribute of God. It is impossible to do otherwise than take one or the other of these alternatives, if you think on the subject at all. O ! that the infamous falsehood of predestination were uprooted from the souls of men. Why should it be held for a moment ? Simply because men refuse to admit that God could create a being whose will should be

* Calvin's Inst. b. iii. ch. xviii. † Conf. ch. iii.

perfectly free, and whose actions should be events truly and absolutely contingent in their nature. Grant Jehovah but this power—the glory of being capable of knowing and causing the absolute freedom of this human soul, and you withdraw from His name the infamy of having caused the sin and death of millions, while He declares on oath that He has no pleasure in the death of any one. Think, my hearer, of the fact, that you must yet feel all your weight for eternity depending upon truth in God, and you will not put this subject readily aside.

6. *Consider the weeping of Jesus on the Mount of Olives.* It is thus recorded by Luke: "And when He was come near, He beheld the city, and wept over it, saying, If [or, O that] thou hadst known, even thou at least in this thy day, the things that belong to thy peace; but now they are hid from thine eyes!" What would be the impression that these tears, and that exclamation, would make upon the mind of an attentive spectator of this scene? Would it not be that the whole heart of this Saviour was yearning over the lost? Would the idea strike the mind that this same Being had ordained to perdition all over whom He was weeping, and that He was so arranging and controlling all things so as to secure the destruction of those over whom He was thus lamenting? If any man can believe the doctrine of reprobation, or of the "*passing by*" of the lost by God, in the face of the weeping Jesus, he can believe also that truth is falsehood, and falsehood truth—that good is evil, and evil good—he can believe any contradiction that it is possible to couch in language. He has in-

deed a gigantic faith. But such a man must account for his faith, and be answerable for its effects. He must yet feel that he has borne his share in that vast corruption of the human mind in which all religion is treated with contempt, or secret aversion, as a mass of the most contradictory absurdities. O! my hearer, let me entreat you to think how you would like to have that conduct ascribed to you, which this doctrine ascribes to God. If you cared a straw for your character as a man of truth, you would regard the wide spread belief that such was your way, as one of the greatest of injuries. Let us rejoice that this horrid dogma of a dying system is so manifestly opposed to the plain truth of God. Let us take *His own* expressions as the index of His heart; and we shall find, that, as is the index, so is every secret thought and design that even eternity itself shall reveal.

What, then, is the conclusion to which we are led by the whole of this subject? Can we longer believe that God has foreordained the destinies of men? Can we believe that His *expressed* mind is no index of His secret will? Must we conclude that, when He weeps over a soul lost, and thus externally expresses the deepest grief at the loss, still, *secretly*, He is quite satisfied with the event, as one of those which He decreed from all eternity for the promotion of His glory? Must not the soul abhor such ideas of God? Must we not feel constrained to renounce forever a creed that is founded on them? Must we not labor to overturn the delusion that has spread itself over our land, slaying it by the sword of the Spirit, which is the word of God?

O! let us realize His love—His deep, earnest, and universal love. Let us fix our minds upon that most glorious display of His love that we have in His sacrifice for the whole world. Let us not overlook His condescention and desire, as the Almighty Spirit, for the world's conversion. Let us remember that, when He says He is resisted, it is really so; and yet He suffers long, and is kind. He continues to strive that the heart of the guilty and ungrateful may be won. Let us dwell upon the heart of our Lord thus revealed; and, freed from the fearful bondage of the idea that all is fixed, let us seek, by the Spirit and Truth of God, to pluck many, who are as yet brands, from the fearful burning. Hearer, you are free to the love of God. All are welcome, for Jesus has died for all, and God is love to all. Be inspired with sympathy, with this universal love, and live to Him who loved you and gave Himself for you.

LECTURE V.

PREDESTINATION AND THE LOVE OF GOD.

The truth by which Jesus Himself brought the mind of Nicodemus to peace and rest, is that which, above all others, expresses the love of God. It has proved the resting-place of many a soul since it was uttered in the hearing of the Jewish ruler; and there is sufficient in it when understood and believed, to be the rest and peace of every soul of man: "God so loved the world, that He gave His only-begotten Son, that whosoever believeth in Him might not perish, but have everlasting life." The spirit and value of this truth depends upon the universality and intensity of the love of God; and the heaviest charge that can be brought against the doctrine of predestination, as generally understood, is that of mangling, and hiding from the dying eye, this blessed remedy for the soul.

Let us, then, in a series of remarks, bring out and confirm this charge against the doctrine in question.

1. *The doctrine of universal predestination hides, most effectually, the unbounded extent of divine love.* That the benevolence or love of God embraces every man, is a truth so involved in the still more glorious truth that "God is love," that it is impossible to believe the one and not, at the same time, to believe the other. How can any one be-

lieve that "GOD IS LOVE," and, at the same time, believe that He is not love to every creature capable of being an object of that affection? God can not, in His nature, and in the essential principle of His mind, be one thing to one man and another thing to another man. He is not double-minded in any sense. This is a most blessed truth; it is, indeed, a treasure to every soul that realizes it. The Lord of Hosts, while He approves of the holy, and in the sense of approval loves only such as are so, is benevolent, and, in this sense, is love—real and unlimited love to all. Hence, not a sinner on the face of the earth requires to be at a loss for a friend. Every created heart might be cold to the outcast, and yet ONE heart is love to him, and that the heart of his God. Thus Jehovah bids us love even our enemies, because He has first set us the example of loving His.

Let us now see how the doctrine of predestination agrees with this. It is most evident that one or other of them must die; they can not both live in one mind. Calvin, remarking on the case of the lost, in connection with that gross mistranslation * that occurs in the common version of Isaiah vi. 9, 10, says, "Observe, He directs His voice to them, but it is that they may become more deaf; He kindles a light, but it is that they may become more blind; He publishes His doctrine, but it is that they may become more besotted; He applies a remedy, but it is that they may not be healed." Now, can any one, believing that passage, also believe that these are objects of divine love? It is impossible.

* See the Lecture on this and its kindred passages.

But mark, this treatment is not the consequence of their sin; it is the declared *cause* of their sin, and the result of God's eternal decree! This treatment, as we have seen from repeated quotations already, is God's making way for the fulfillment of His decrees. How, then, is it possible for those holding this idea to believe that "God is love" to those who are thus treated? It is absolutely impossible; and thus one of the most glorious truths in the universe is banished from the mind. We may illustrate and prove the truth of this remark by looking into the views of those who advocate the doctrine now in hand. There is, for example, one most extraordinary way of meeting this argument against predestination, as generally held, which I met with lately. It is found in the following words, and is supposed to prove the universality of divine love: "To say, as some do, that the atonement, if held to be undertaken for a certain number, can not be a demonstration of love to all, is to confound the secret with the revealed will of God. Were the parties, whether few or many, for whom it is undertaken, named in the proclamation of it, it could not be a demonstration of good-will to mankind generally, or to sinners indiscriminately, as such. But, since what is revealed is simply the way of acceptance, or the principle on which God acts in justifying the ungodly, it seems plain, that to whomsoever such a revelation comes, with names and numbers suppressed, it is, in its very nature, a revelation of love."[*] What, then, is the love of God, that is love to all? This author tells us that it is love that

[*] Candlish on the Atonement, pp. 19, 20.

depends for its existence, even in appearance, on the *suppression* of the truth. And what do men generally think of love that requires, even for existence in appearance, the suppression of truth? What do they understand by love that would cease even to appear to be, the moment the whole secret of the heart is revealed? They think it love in *name* only, and generally call it hypocrisy. I doubt if ever a more fatal passage was penned in defense of limiting decrees, than that which we have quoted. It is *fatal* to the doctrine it is intended to defend. The writer is compelled to admit the universality of God's love, and he confesses, with great simplicity, that the best love to all, of which his doctrine admits, is love that depends for its demonstration on the suppression of names and numbers! Surely, the time will come when such confessions will have their due weight with men. Only think of the effect which it would have on the character of an advocate who pretended to defend a criminal at the bar, if he frankly admitted that the demonstration of the innocence of him whose cause he advocated depended in the suppression of "names and numbers!" Would not innocence be in a sad predicament in the hands of such a pleader? And where is the love of God in the hands of the pleader before us? He admits that its demonstration depends on the suppression of "names and numbers"—his doctrine compels him to make the admission—what, then, are we to think of the doctrine? Is it from God? No. Let us rejoice, my hearer, that it is not. Neither does nature, nor does Providence, nor does the Bible, speak such fearful absurdity of God. These great and consistent expounders of the heart of our Father combine their energies of expression, to convey to our minds, with the greatest possible force, the blessed reality that "God is love" to every creature He has formed; and that He so loved the world of men as to give up His most precious gift to be a sacrifice for its sins, that not one soul might want a clear way back to the bosom from which it had strayed. God's heart needs no concealment. No. Could you see its utmost depth—could you know its most secret sentiment—and could you open and read the book of His most mysterious decrees, and have all Jehovah before your mind, you would only be more deeply and overpoweringly impressed with the sentiment, that "GOD IS LOVE." Rejoice that this truth shall yet rise, by the steady power of God Himself, above all the rubbish that the error of ages has thrown upon it, and shine forth before the eyes of the world like the sun in his strength. My hearer, be it yours to come near to the heart of your God: His heart and hand are bending and stretched out toward you now. O! be assured of His boundless love.

2. *The doctrine in question hides the true intensity of the love of God.* It represents God as dealing with human nature very much in the way in which a careless potter would deal with a piece of clay—making it into vessels, some of which were of no use but to be destroyed, and others to various other purposes. This idea of the potter and the clay is a Scripture one; but the beauty of the Bible truth is entirely defaced by the character that is

given to the potter. In the Bible, he is one who makes the most of every means in order to form the clay, and all the clay into vessels of honor. In the doctrine of those who advocate predestination he puts the clay upon the wheel *at first*, with a determination that a great part of it will be made into vessels for destruction. This is not like God. We shall take one Scriptural illustration of the intensity of the love of God toward the lost. In Luke xv. we have an account of Jesus charged as being "the friend of sinners." Read there His three parables of the lost sheep, the lost piece of money, and the lost son. Think of the feelings of the shepherd who lost his sheep, or those of the woman who lost the money, or of the father of the prodigal—all of which are taken to show the nature of the feelings of God. Think if they can possibly agree with the idea of God as one who decreed from all eternity the everlasting destruction of millions of souls, and who did this purely of His own will. The shepherd is so intensely interested in the lost sheep, that he comparatively forgets the ninety-and-nine that are left. If this be a fair representation of God, can the foreordination of men to wrath, or the "passing by" of the greater portion of them, be true? It is impossible. Here, again, we see that one of the two doctrines must be given up. We can not both hold the infinite intensity of God's love to souls, and believe that He can treat them in this way. This is an argument that tells against all forms of limiting the grace of God. It is no more possible to reconcile it with the idea of sinners "passed by," than with that of sinners "ordained to wrath."

3. *The doctrine in question overlooks the true nature of the love of God.* It takes for granted that God may be love to one being and not to another. Now, while this is true of His complacency in a holy being, it is false of His benevolence, or true and unchangeable love. It is true that He delights to contemplate holiness, and that He abhors sin, and in this sense loves no unholy being whatever; but it is not with *this* love that the doctrine of predestination interferes in any way whatever: it is with the truth regarding the benevolence or compassion—or real love of the heart of God. The doctrine regards this love as an *exercise*, rather than a changeless attribute of the divine mind. It places love in God in the same position as that which we find it occupying in man,—that is, we find man *capable* of loving merely—we do not find love to be a changeless attribute of his nature. We, therefore, find him capable of loving one and hating another—of having compassion for one, and no compassion for another, who is equally requiring his compassion. Love with man is thus a mere changeable exercise of the mind; and hence it would be false to say of any man, he "is love." But this is the Bible description of the moral nature of God: it is the most glorious truth in the universe—"God is love." This is, indeed, the fountain from which that universe has sprung, and from which all the wants of that universe are supplied. Now, how can God, who is love, be, in this love, one thing to one man which He is not to another? How can

He possess one changeless attribute of character—an attribute which is the sum of all the rest? How can He possess this when contemplating one case of sin and misery, and not possess it when He contemplates another? The fact is, that we *must* give up the idea that "*God is love*" in its full meaning, and in every truly glorious meaning that we can conceive, if we hold the doctrine of universal predestination. How can we hold that of two men, equally guilty and helpless, God will pity and love the one, and determine him for heaven, and not pity nor love the other, and determine him, out of His mere will, for hell! How is it conceivable that a man can have the true idea of Jehovah's love, and such a doctrine in his mind's belief at the same time! It is absolutely impossible. We may grant the possibility of His making a declaration of the belief of both *in words*, but we can not grant his actually possessing in His mind both ideas.

Only contrast the two. "God is love," infinite, unchangeable, universal love—love to every being because unchangeable love in His own heart itself. Take this glorious truth along with the following: "Now, with respect to the reprobate, whom the apostle introduces in the same place; as Jacob without any merit, yet obtained by good works, is made an object of grace: so Esau, while yet unpolluted by any crime, is accounted an object of hatred." Again,—"Lastly, He subjoins a concluding observation, that God hath mercy on whom He will have mercy, and whom He will he hardeneth. You see how He attributes both to the mere will of God. If, therefore, we can assign no reason why He grants mercy to His people but because such is His pleasure, neither shall we find any other cause but His will for the reprobation of others. For when God is said to harden or show mercy to whom He pleases, men are brought, by this declaration, to seek *no cause besides His will.*" * Here, then, is Jacob and Esau, yet unborn—both helpless objects —unborn infants. Jehovah is represented as looking upon the two; and, merely because He so wills, He loves the one and hates the other! And, my hearer, does this accord with your ideas of the truth that "God is love?" I venture to affirm, that you will as soon create a world as you will hold both of these ideas as portions of the belief of your mind at the same time. Is it not, then, indubitably evident, that the one doctrine destroys the other? You must surrender one of them;—which shall it be? the doctrine that "*God is love*," or the doctrine that is *infinitely opposed to that idea?* O! it is surely not difficult to choose between the two. There is surely enough of humanity—fallen humanity in the one, and enough of manifest divinity in the other, to determine the choice.

4. *The doctrine in question throws suspicion upon the reality of divine love altogether.* We shall see the force of this remark if we take the case of a father of a family. Let us suppose that he has born to him two children—*twins*. Let us suppose that he looks upon these little helpless ones the first time they are presented to him, and he loves the one and hates the other. What should we think of such love? Should we set it down as

* Calvin's Institutes.

real undoubted compassion and kindness of heart, or infamous and most capricious favoritism? I leave my hearer to answer. Mark, we are not *permitted* to suppose that this father found any reason in the two children why he preferred the one to the other. He just *willed* to love the one and to hate the other. And is this love?—is this real love?—is this all the love that we are to ascribe to our God?—love that can thus WILL to embrace one UNBORN INFANT and reject another. Let the question ring in the ears, and trouble the soul of the man who will yield to prejudice instead of the truth of God; and let him never rest until he answer it. No favorite can possibly regard the favoritism by which he is distinguished from his equally deserving and equally helpless and needy neighbor, with the reverence that is paid in the inmost soul to real love. No man can be truly devoted to the doctrine of universal predestination, as we have quoted it in the words of one of its greatest advocates, and at the same time be deeply imbued with the influence of divine love. If his heart is to be devoted to the one, he must desert the other. The very reality of divine love must be sacrificed in the mind, or the doctrine in question must be dismissed. O! then, my hearer, think not that, as a practical question, the one now before us is of small moment. Thousands are under the full influence of that horrid doctrine; and because they are so, they fail entirely to perceive and realize the love of God. They are living as if they were the subjects of a capricious, and, it may be to them, a cold-hearted king. The great calumniator of God is doing his utmost to strengthen the error and perpetuate the delusion. Who is not bound to do his utmost to burst the spell by the destruction of the *truth* regarding God? If we are "not our own, but bought with a price, even the precious blood of Christ," and thus bound to "glorify God in our bodies and spirits, which are His," surely we are, above all, bound to use both these bodies and spirits in seeking to clear His name from this most fearful stain. Understand, then, for yourselves, and be prepared thus to be the means in God's hand of removing the delusions of your fellow-men. Let your soul drink deep into the fountain of divine love, that out of the fullness of your heart, your lips may speak of Jehovah.

5. *The doctrine in question hides one of the most glorious displays of the love of God.* Next to the redemption of man by the sacrifice of Jesus, the creation of a being truly free stands prominent as a display of divine love. We see benevolence in the existence and wonderful construction of the whole inanimate creation. We see more love in the creation of animate, though irrational and instinctive beings. We see the greatest of all creation's displays of love in the constitution of those who are fitted to bear the image of God Himself as free spirits. "*Freedom*" is a word that sounds sweetly in the ears of every man of right mind, and the creation of real and perfect freedom—of liberty unconstrained—is truly worthy of God. Now, under the hands of the advocates of universal predestination, what does freedom become to man?—what, especially, the freedom of the eternally reprobate,

who are "created to shame and death eternal?" If it is freedom at all, it is that of the prey in the power of the destroyer. It may be allowed to run and sport for a moment or two, but its doom is fixed. Lest it should be supposed, again, that my language is too strong, and that I load the doctrine with inferences of my own, let its great advocate speak for himself. What are we to understand by the following words?—"Nor should it be thought absurd to affirm, that God not only foresaw the fall of the first man, and the ruin of his posterity in him, but also arranged all by the determination of His own will." Again,—"Those, therefore, whom He hath created to a life of shame and death of destruction, that they might be instruments of His wrath, and examples of His severity, *He causes* to reach their appointed end." This is the "*freedom*" of predestination. Does it illustrate the love of God? Is it a prominent example of glorious love? Is not all dark around the love of God, when you look to such a representation of His dealings? Do you not find it necessary to exclaim, "Mystery! mystery!" when such a view is presented to your mind. Yes, it *is* a mystery how such a position as that said to be occupied by the reprobate can be that of a free creature; and how the freedom enjoyed by him can be a fruit of love. Once more, it is most evident, that he who holds the love of God in the creation of man, can not hold the doctrine of universal predestination. He who would see the *infinite* glory of that kind thought in the mind of Jehovah, that grew up to the design of calling into existence a race of beings capable of bearing His own image—of entering into the joys of His holiness, and of existing as long as Himself —ruling upon their thrones for ever,—he who would see the incalculable love of that thought, must reject, for ever, the ideas we have just quoted.

But on this point we must go further. It involves redemption of man as well as his creation. Where was the LOVE of the sacrifice of Jesus, if that sacrifice was not made to gain the hearts of FREE creatures, and still to retain untouched their native liberty? Where was the necessity for that *sacrifice*, if all things are according to the *real*, though *secret*, will of Jehovah? If we are to see love, must it only be that of Him who first of all decrees a calamity, and arranges so that it must come, and then makes a sacrifice to remedy that which He Himself has decreed? Would it not, we may well ask, be love rather to refrain from decreeing the evil at first? This may be called replying against God. I answer, it is replying against that God who acts in the way described in the quotations I have made; but I utterly deny that it is replying against the God of the Bible. This refuge is just a miserable "begging of the question." Prove first that God actually did determine the guilt of man, and afterward made a sacrifice to atone for that which He had Himself decreed; and *then* charge him who finds fault with replying against God. Look, then, at the two ideas. God, whose heart of love led Him to create a FREE spirit—that spirit abusing freedom, and against every desire and design of God, committing sin—God then making an infinitely costly sacrifice to atone for that sin, and reclaim this free creature to Himself. This is love. Look at the other side. God creating a creature under desire to sin; so arranging as to bring about that sin; and *then* making a sacrifice to atone for it. Which of these two ideas are to be preferred? It is impossible for any man to plead misrepresentation here. If he does, how can we fairly represent the views of men but by quoting their own words? O! my hearer, see the true glory of your God. See that glory, as the glory of love, in His creating us free creatures. See our own unfathomable guilt in sinning against such a Creator. See, then, His love in atoning, to His own holy and righteous government, for our sins, and condescending to reinstate us in our lost privileges, as His own free and forgiven children! Be led to adore His love. Drink deep into this blessed and refreshing truth, and be prepared to overwhelm any idea that is contrary to it, by the clearness and fullness of your views of the heart of your God. Darkness may contend with darkness, and the issue may be victory to either side, or success to none; but, bring the love of God, as displayed in the truth of His word, to bear upon error, and the issue can not be doubtful.

6. *The doctrine in question proceeds upon the idea that God is* LOVE OF FAME *instead of* LOVE ITSELF. This, indeed, is the fundamental principle of the system to which the doctrine is essential. Now, it is quite true that every thing that God does glorifies Him, and it is true that His *real glory* is the most important and essential object

that can be promoted in the universe. It is true, therefore, that He does nothing but what is fitted to promote that glory. This is true, not because the supreme and truly glorious principle of His character is love of glory; but because that principle is holy love itself. There is all the difference between love ever glorifying itself, because ever acting consistently with itself, and a being sacrificing others merely to glorify His own name—all the difference that is between God and a tyrant of the worst character. Now, mark the force of the following description of God. The doctrine defended is, that He had predestinated millions from eternity to be eternally lost. It may be stated, in the words of its own advocates,—" That the reprobate obey not the word of God, when made known to them, is justly imputed to the wickedness and depravity of their hearts, PROVIDED it be at the same time stated, that they are abandoned to this depravity, *because they have been raised up, by a just but inscrutable judgment of God*, to display His glory in their condemnation." * Such a statement as this naturally gives rise to the question, " *Did God make men for the purpose of condemning them ?* " Hear how this question is answered: " God made man—every man, and every thing, to glorify Him." Again, " If the question is asked, 'Did God make the devil and his angels only to damn them?' I answer, He made them for His own glory." † This, then, is the doctrine:—God creates men, whom from all eternity He has fore-

---

* Calvin's Inst., book iii. chap. xxiv.
† Truth and Error, p. 45.

ordained to condemnation; but, as it is His object to glorify Himself by this, we are not to say that He made them merely to condemn them. He made them for condemnation only as a means to an end, and that end, His own fame. Now, it is impossible to understand men's words at all, if those words we have quoted do not convey the idea that God eternally determined to create men for eternal death, that thereby He might have glory. Is not this just the character that we have in the so-called hero, who sees that the sacrifice of a hundred men is essential to his fame, and he orders them to meet death? By his irresistible word, he appoints them that part of the field in which they must die, to sustain or promote his fame! God is set before us as fixing His eternal decrees—He writes down one million for life, to glorify His mercy, but He must have another million to glorify His power and justice, and He writes down these for death. We are not to question the correctness of the representation, because He writes down both for His glory! O, infamous libel upon that most spotless heart of infinite and universal love! How is it possible that such an idea should ever possess the minds of ransomed men! What must be their ideas of *glory*, who hold such an idea of God! What glory could arise to *justice* from the condemnation of men who had been created under a decree unalterably fixing their shame and death! These three words, GOD IS LOVE, ought to banish such doctrines for ever from the minds of men. All the arguments that a sophistical ingenuity ever invented, are crushed before that omnipotent and all-embracing truth. O! my hearer, know that God regards every sin as His *dishonor*. Every breaker of the law dishonors Him; and, if He had foreordained sin, He would have foreordained His own dishonor, and not His glory. If He had foreordained sin, His punishment of that which He had decreed Himself, would have been His deepest dishonor, instead of His glory. But He decreed *against* sin. Every thing that He could do consistently with maintaining the freedom of man, He did and decreed, in order to prevent sin, and render unnecessary the condemnation of man. On this ground we do see that condemnation is to His glory. It is honorable to dispense needful justice, and so to uphold the benevolent laws of the universe; but even this glory would be extinguished, if it were true that God had foreordained sin.

What more is needful in order to our most hearty renunciation of that doctrine which so fearfully reverses the character of God? Were our own character, or that of some dear friend, so treated as the character of God has been, how should we feel and act? We could not be indifferent. We could not be passive in the matter. We could not think our best and noblest energies misspent in the work of needed vindication. Let me, then, earnestly exhort the hearer to have his own soul lighted up with the true glory of divine love. Let him have his whole spirit filled by sympathy with the compassion of Jehovah. Let him drink deep into the stream of living water, that he may be refreshed with the spirit of love and of truth, and then do his utmost for the clearing of the character and true glory of God. O! my friend, you can not comprehend the vast importance of what is thus before you. Eternity alone will show how momentous is the work to which you are thus called.

LECTURE VI.

PREDESTINATION AND THE CRUCIFIXION OF JESUS.

In the five foregoing lectures our attention has been chiefly confined to the bearing of the attributes of God on the doctrine of predestination. Now we must turn to the consideration of those parts of His word which are quoted in support of the idea, that every thing that takes place is predetermined of God Himself. I rejoice to contemplate this part of our important subject. It will be seen that, where dark and darkening views of the glory of our great Lord have been given, as the truth revealed in the texts, many of the most encouraging illustrations of His love have been buried beneath the comments of men.

The first passage to which we shall turn is that in which the death of Jesus is said to have been the result of the decree of God. Acts iv. 27–28:— "For of a truth against thy holy child Jesus, whom thou hast anointed, both Herod and Pontius Pilate, with the Gentiles and the people of Israel, were gathered together, for to do whatsoever thy hand and thy counsel had determined before to be done." This text is supposed to furnish indubitable evidence that God hath "foreordained *whatsoever* comes to pass." It is taken as ground for the statement that "the deeds of these wicked men" (the murderers of Jesus) are said to have come to pass according to "the counsel of God."* This text, then, is thus supposed to teach emphatically the foreordination of sin itself. Let us consider it as thus understood.

I. WHAT CONSTITUTED THE NECESSITY OF PREDESTINATION IN THE MATTER OF JESUS' DEATH?

This is a most important question, inasmuch as its answer will show us the impossibility of God's predestinating wicked deeds in any circumstances.

1. *I answer, that sin alone constituted the necessity of the death and sacrifice of Jesus.* Is it possible that this can be denied? Is it conceivable that any desire of God's heart would have brought about the sacrifice of His most Beloved had it not been for sin? Suppose that no sin had been foreseen of God, and that thus no sin had existed in the universe, is it conceivable that such a thing as the death of His Son should have been decreed of God? Well, then, we see clearly the *cause*, and the *sole* and *first cause* of the sacrifice of Jesus. We see the necessity that called for it, and that necessity is, simply, wicked deeds on the part of men.

2. *We can not find the first necessity for the death of Jesus in any of the attributes of God, unless we view these in the light in which they are affected by sin.* It is true that the *love* of Jehovah gave up His Son to die for man; but why was this love called upon to do so? What cried out to that love to come forth with such a costly sacrifice? I answer, SIN. But for this, that love would sooner have ceased to be, than have made such a sacrifice.

* Truth and Error, p. 54.

It is also true that the *justice* of God demanded the sacrifice of Jesus. But why was this demand ever made by justice? The answer is, because of SIN. If this had not existed, justice must have become injustice before it could have *permitted* the death of Jesus. It is clear, then, that not only is sin the cause of Jesus' death, but that all the attributes of God would have combined to prevent that death but for this very sin. Now, keep this most important fact in view, and see if you can admit that even this sin has been predetermined of God. Mark this well, for if sin be not foreordained, then it is not true that whatsoever comes to pass is so.

II. CONSIDER SOME OF THE MOST OBVIOUS OBJECTIONS THAT LIE AGAINST PREDESTINATED SIN IN CONNECTION WITH THE DEATH OF JESUS.

Every man must be conscious, on reflection, that there is something of an inexplicable nature in the idea of sin being foreordained of God. Even those that hold it, state it in such a way as to show that their minds are not at ease on the subject, and those who wish to adhere to it are generally most deeply grieved at its being drawn forth for consideration.

1. *The doctrine that sin is predestinated by God involves the idea that God Himself gave rise to the necessity for the death of His Son.* Since it must be held that sin alone called for the death of Jesus, if it is held also that this sin is the result of God's decree, then it *inevitably* follows that God Himself decreed the only cause in the universe for

the death of His Son. In "the glorious gospel of the blessed God" we are taught that "God so loved the world that He gave His Son;" but how does this look, if we are told that, had He not foreordained sin, that gift would never have been needed by the world? Where is the love, in first causing the calamity, and then providing a remedy for it? Oh, my hearer! you may be one of those who, by their countenance and support in various forms, hold up before the world the doctrine, that even sin is foreordained,—if you are, let me most solemnly warn you of the fearful consequences of being called to account for this support. By holding forth to the world this fearful error, you are depriving the love of God of all its glory, and men of all the benefit to be found for them in that wondrous love.

2. *The doctrine of predestinated sin involves the idea that God gave up Jesus to destroy what He Himself has decreed.* The object of Jesus is said to have been, "to destroy the works of the devil." The doctrine before us would make it appear that He came to destroy that which He Himself had foreordained. Surely nothing can be plainer than that if He foreordained sin—if He decreed it to be as it is—and came to die to destroy it—His death was endured to destroy His own decreed object. How can we escape from this but by denying that sin is decreed at all? How can we deny that sin is decreed, but by also renouncing the doctrine we have been taught from our infancy, that God hath "foreordained whatsoever comes to pass?" Especially must we renounce the doctrine that the wicked

deeds of the murderers of Jesus were decreed of God. Were we to admit this, what would we make of the parable of the husbandmen, in which the murder of Jesus is shown to be the most fearful of crimes? Only read the following verses, and try if you can conceive of a secret decree ordaining that the husbandmen should kill the son of the lord of the vineyard:—" Then began He to speak to the people this parable: A certain man planted a vineyard, and let it forth to husbandmen, and went into a far country for a long time. And at the season he sent a servant to the husbandmen, that they should give him of the fruit of the vineyard; but the husbandmen beat him, and sent him away empty. And again he sent another servant: and they beat him also, and entreated him shamefully, and sent him away empty. And again he sent a third; and they wounded him also, and cast him out. Then said the lord of the vineyard, What shall I do? I will send my beloved son: it may be they will reverence him when they see him. But when the husbandmen saw him, they reasoned among themselves, saying, This is the heir; come, let us kill him, that the inheritance may be ours. So they cast him out of the vineyard, and killed him. What, therefore, shall the lord of the vineyard do unto them? He shall come and destroy these husbandmen, and shall give the vineyard to others. And when they heard it, they said, God forbid." Luke xx. 9-16. If the lord of that vineyard secretly decreed the wickedness of these men, and so arranged that they should certainly bring about the murder of his son—if all that sin was the fulfillment of his prearranged plans—on what conceivable principle can you vindicate the course pursued in their destruction? But you will now be prepared to urge the explanation of the text before us.

III. What, then, is the meaning of this most important verse?

I have dwelt on the objections that lie against the too common view entertained of the passage, in order that the honestly inquiring mind may thirst for the right view. There are too many disposed just to take any view that may be presented to them, if it only come from high authority, and be stated with sufficient confidence. I have shown that it is impossible to hold that the wicked deeds of the murderers of Jesus were foreordained of God, and at the same time hold to His love and justice as displayed in the gift of Jesus. This should dispose men to seek a better view.

1. *The whole Bible teaches us that sin came into this world in defiance of God.* If we carefully study every expression of God in regard to sin, we shall see that He regards it as the accursed intrusion, of responsible and guilty creatures, upon His holy plans. It is indeed out of the question to pretend to prove the sincerity of His threatenings against it but on this ground.

2. *A remedy was required for the case of the guilty.* An atonement was required for sin, or there could be no forgiveness. The heart of God was set upon men. He hated infinitely their sin, but He

infinitely loved their souls. This unbounded love needed the atonement—it required a ransom, that it might deliver from going down to the pit. The ransom must be a victim worthy and able to die as an acceptable substitute for guilty men. One being in the universe, and one alone, could be accepted, and that was the Son of God. "God so loved the world that He gave His Son." That He might destroy sin, He did not consider the sacrifice too great, nor did He grudge the cost in His love to man. His best gift was surrendered to be a curse for us all, that we might be delivered from sin.

3. *We are told, in another passage of the Acts of the Apostles, what Jehovah decreed.* His decree was not kept a secret (chap. iii. 18), "But those things which God before had showed by the mouths of all His prophets, *that Christ should suffer*, He hath so fulfilled." This teaches us that the decree of Jehovah was the decree that Jesus should suffer —not that man should be so wicked as to murder Him. Any one may distinguish, surely, between God decreeing the sufferings of Jesus and His decreeing the sins of men. It is clearly stated here, that it was the *sufferings* and not the sins that was declared beforehand. O! there is infinite love in the *real* decree—that even if sin existed, and could not be forgiven but through the sufferings of His beloved Son, He should decree the accursed death of Jesus for man. "Herein is love;" but dark is the picture, indeed, when we hear, that the SIN for which this death was suffered, was decreed. Blessed be the God of the Bible, He has not darkened the glorious truth. Mark, my hearer, that

God's declared decree was not that men should be wicked, but that Jesus should suffer for that wickedness which men had brought in upon the holy plans and purposes of Jehovah.

4. *God foresaw the wickedness of the Jews and Romans at the time of the death of Jesus.* We have already been able to distinguish between foreseeing and fore-fixing. It is not difficult to do so. We see most clearly that God *foreknew* and *foretold* the state of mind in which the murderers of Jesus would be at this particular time. He foresaw the treatment that Jesus would receive if surrendered into their hands. No one can doubt this. No one can feel any difficulty with this truth. Admitting that God not only sees all that will take place, but also all that *might* take place on other conditions, we perceive clearly that all along He knew, that if the holy Jesus was delivered into the hands of these men, He would suffer the most fearful death they could possibly inflict upon Him. Now, observe, God had determined that Jesus should suffer —He had declared this determination from the day on which man sinned; and He foresaw that the wickedness of man would be so great, that were Jesus delivered into their hands, the very sacrifice required would be made. All this is infinitely removed from the idea that God foreordained sin. Perfect light is not more opposite to perfect darkness, than these ideas are opposite to each other; and the word of God carries us fully out in the affirmation of the one and the denial of the other.

5. *The decree as to how Jesus should suffer, and as to the part Jehovah should bear in the scenes*

of Calvery, are clearly stated in another passage of this same book. Acts ii. 23 :—" Him being DELIVERED by the determinate counsel and foreknowledge of God, ye have taken, and by wicked hands have crucified and slain." Now, mark the force of that text. What is the decree of God declared to be? THE SURRENDER OF JESUS INTO WICKED HANDS. God had determined by His hand and His counsel, that Jesus should suffer death for the sins of men. He foresaw that, if surrendered into the hands of the wicked, He would suffer that death; and He determined to surrender Him. I appeal to the conscience of every hearer, if this is not the truth taught in these passages. In the name of that God who has been slandered by the imputation of decreeing wicked deeds, I challenge mankind to show that these passages say more than that He determined that Jesus should suffer and be crucified; and foreseeing that He should suffer if surrendered to the hands of men, He determined so to surrender Him. It may be thought that I speak strongly—it may be, too strongly. Let it be remembered that it is declared, that unless we "*explain away*" these texts, we must admit the predestination of sin. This is declared by men that are bound, by all the ties that can oblige humanity, to labor for the vindication of God. O! then, my hearer, let me beseech you to study these three passages, and do your utmost, and see if you can find the predestination of sin in them.

6. *Let us notice particularly the force of the passage principally mentioned.* Herod and the rest were gathered together to do whatsoever God had

determined by His hand and counsel to be done. Is not the natural question—*what* had He determined to be done? And is not the scriptural answer, that He had determined that Christ should suffer? And how did He determine that this should be done? The answer of the Bible again is, He determined that Jesus should suffer by being delivered into the hands of wicked men. Here, again, all is clear. Let us suppose that a man is met and surrounded by robbers, who demand his money or his life. Let us suppose that, in order to save his life, he surrenders his property; is he to be looked upon as the cause of the necessity that came upon him; or if he say that he determined to deliver his money into the hands of the robbers, is this to be understood as if he had determined the whole matter of the robbery? Or, if he, having foreseen the robbery, determined to take advantage of it for some great and good purpose, and declared his determination to do so, would it be fair to construe this into a determination of the wicked act of robbery itself, and of all that is done with the money after? No more can it be just (because God foresaw the wickedness of the murderers of Jesus, and declared His determination to deliver Him into their hands, and thus to accomplish the needed sacrifice and atonement) to say that He decreed that wickedness, in the exercise of which Jesus was slain.

In concluding our consideration of these passages, and of the foreordination of the death of Jesus, let us mark the simplicity and glory of the ways of God, when the doctrine of universal foreordination is rejected. He forms a holy host of free and immortal beings. He makes every arrangement consistent with the natures that He has thus formed, to lead them on in purity and love. A portion of these creatures disobey and willfully trample on the divine and holy plan of God. They are punished according to law. Another portion of His holy creation are led to sin, and also to trample upon the holy and infinitely benevolent designs of the Lord. He sees it possible, by making a sacrifice, the most costly the universe can furnish, to ransom them from the righteous sentence of outraged justice. He sees that this sacrifice can be made by simply delivering up the precious victim to the hands of the wicked, for whom He is to die; and He determines to do this—to make this surrender. Hence, the "power" of Pilate. Jesus is delivered into the hands of ready murderers. This surrender is God's determination carried out. O! my hearer, can you not see the wisdom and love of your God in this? Immense, surely, is the difference between this view of Him, and that which is given when He is represented as foreordaining the sin for which Christ died. Let me earnestly beseech you to look upon your God as represented by Himself, and all your darkness will be banished before the rich glory of His most consistent ways. Be assured that you will be most abundantly rewarded for every hour of earnest and prayerful study that you devote to the character of your God. Let not your precious opportunities pass without the most faithful and diligent improvement. Dig into the mine of divine truth, guided by the leadings of the Spirit of God; as you take first the simplest and plainest of His lessons—go forward and you will find that "God is light, and in Him is no darkness at all." You will find that His decrees, even the most secret of them, are all such as to inspire your soul with confidence —to humble it under a sense of its own nothingness and sinfulness, and to open and expand the affections of the immortal spirit, till they embrace Jehovah, and all created beings, with deep, and earnest, and Christ-like love.

LECTURE VII.

PREDESTINATION AND GOD'S PURPOSE IN JESUS.

The passage to which I request your attention in this lecture is found in Paul's second epistle to Timothy, ch. i: 9 :—"Who hath saved us, and called us with an holy calling, not according to our works, but according to His own purpose and grace, which was given us, in Christ Jesus, before the world began." This is a passage of great interest, inasmuch as, in its connection, it shows the universal bearing of the purpose of God in regard to Jesus. I shall not enter into all the subjects presented to the mind in the passage, but principally confine your attention to the purpose and grace said to be given, in Christ Jesus, before the world began. The consideration of this will afford a blessed opportunity of studying the glorious gospel in one of its aspects of universal love.

I. WHAT PURPOSE AND GRACE ARE HERE SPOKEN OF?

The answer to this question forms the key to the full understanding of the whole passage. We can not, therefore, feel too grateful for the kindness of our God, seeing that He has made it an *open* purpose, and that from the time when He gave it; and also, that He has given us, in this connection, the most clear indication of the nature of the purpose to which He refers.

1. *Observe that the purpose and grace here alluded to are no longer secret.* The apostle says that they were *given* at a former time, but he also says that now they are "*manifest*" v. 10—" But is now MADE MANIFEST." Such is the plain declaration of Paul regarding this purpose and grace. You see, then, that these can no longer be regarded as *secret*, and that to understand this passage as referring to a secret purpose, is clearly to misunderstand this portion of God's word. We are shut up, then, to the conclusion, that, whatever this purpose and grace may be, they can not now be secret. That which is "made manifest" can not be secret. Mark this, my hearer, as it is most important to our seeing the full riches of this blessed passage, in contrast with the contracted view given of it by most of ordinary commentators. They will have it to be God's *secret* decree of certain men to life, and this as carried out in the salvation of some, while others are left to perish. This we see it can not be, and we shall see it yet much more fully from this same passage.

2. *Observe that the purpose and grace here spoken of are not made manifest by the conversion of men.* That this purpose is made manifest by conversion is a too common idea. As an objection to what I have already said, it may be urged that it is true the purpose was no longer a secret, so far as Paul and Timothy were concerned; for it was made manifest in their conversion. By their holy lives it was made manifest, that God had eternally decreed

their salvation. Now, mark, that Paul had no idea of this kind before his mind; for, instead of saying that the purpose was made manifest by their conversion, he declares that it was made manifest *before* either of them had shown any signs of conversion. It was "made manifest by the appearing of our Lord Jesus Christ." This is Paul's declaration. Now, what was Paul and what was Timothy when Jesus appeared? Was it *manifest* then that they were the elect of God? Every one knows that the very opposite was manifest. They were then "the children of wrath, even as others." How clearly, then, does it appear, that those are wrong who suppose that the purpose here spoken of is that of election! The fact that learned men should soberly pen such a gross mistake of the meaning of the passage, shows the crying necessity that exists for those who have immortal souls to save, thinking for themselves. What, then, we still ask, was the purpose and grace given in Christ Jesus before the world began? I humbly trust that my hearer is now satisfied that these can not be the purpose and grace of God's determination to call certain persons from among men. What are we to understand, then, by the phrase, the "purpose and grace given?"

3. *Observe that the "*PURPOSE*" and its actual accomplishment must agree.* The purpose is the purpose of that which is now accomplished; and hence both are the same thing viewed in different stages. What, then, was it, the accomplishment of which made manifest, in this case, the purpose of God? If a man has a purpose in his mind, and

keeps it a secret until the accomplishment of its purpose makes it evident what that purpose was, we at once declare the purpose to have been *his determination to do that which he has done.* Now, before us we have a case exactly similar. God's purpose, it is true, was not secret, but it was obscure to many minds, until it was made manifest by the doing of that which He had purposed. What, then, was accomplished? Jesus appeared—He abolished death—He brought life and immortality to light, through the gospel of His death and resurrection. (See verse 10.) This was the work done, and this, the apostle declares, made the purpose manifest. Is it not clear, then, that the purpose was God's purpose, to send Jesus that He might abolish death, and bring life and immortality to light, through the gospel? Yes, my hearer, *this is the purpose,* and this is the grace here spoken of—Jehovah's most gracious purpose to send Jesus to destroy death, and bring life and immortality to light before the eyes of men, by the gospel. Can you not see something infinitely more glorious in this, than in the ideas that have been grafted on the passage—the ideas of God selecting, secretly and partially, a few from among men, and making manifest His partial purpose by picking them out from the crowd! O! what a contrast between the purpose made manifest by the gracious appearing of Jesus Christ, and that made manifest in such a doctrine. There is all the difference between them that there is between a decree invented by man and ascribed to God—and God's infinite heart and mind of all-embracing love. His decree was to give His

Son to die for the world, that whosoever believeth in Him might not perish, but have everlasting life.

4. *There can be no doubt, then, that the purpose here spoken of, is God's purpose of the atonement of Jesus.* This was most unquestionably that which was manifest by the appearing and victorious death of Jesus. It is indeed impossible for any man to imagine any other meaning that the passage can have, if he read it in connection: "His own purpose and grace which was given us in Christ Jesus before the world began, but is now made manifest by the appearing of Jesus Christ." How can you understand these words? To what purpose can they possibly refer? On what conceivable principle of *perversion* can you make them apply to a purpose that, even suppose it had existed as you imagine, could not possibly be made manifest by the appearing of Jesus? And yet men *will* hold that this is God's purpose of converting certain individuals of the human race! Let them hold it, if they are resolved to do so at all hazards. My hearer, turn *you* to the book of God, and read for yourself; and then, even in the verse before you, you will see what God's purpose is. It is the determination that Jesus should appear and abolish death. How did He abolish the death of the soul, that stood as a dark and dreadful sentence between your soul and God? I answer—for God answers—by dying that death in your stead. He abolished the sentence, that stood demanding execution in the eternal ruin of your soul, by becoming a curse for you. He took upon Him part of the flesh and blood, "that *through death* He might destroy him

that had the power of death, that is the devil, and deliver them who, through fear of death, were all their lifetime subject to bondage." How plain is the word of God! How can you mistake the true nature of the purpose made manifest by the appearing of Jesus? O! see how different it is from the purpose which it has often been supposed to be!

5. *Observe that the purpose here spoken of was* "GIVEN *before the times of the ages.*" This is the literal rendering of the apostle's words—"Before the times of the ages," that is, before the dispensations, or at the commencement of the history of the world. In order to see the *time* alluded to, attend first to the fact that the purpose was "given." Now, on what principle can we understand a secret purpose as a purpose given to men? When one man gives a purpose to another, does he not *state* his determination? How else can he be said to give his neighbor his purpose? The whole idea, therefore, of a *secret* purpose, vanishes from this portion of the Bible. It is a *given* purpose, and a given purpose can not be a *secret* one.

In order to the full confirmation of this truth, and also to the understanding of the phrase, "the times of the ages," it is only necessary to look to the Epistle of Titus, ch. i. ver. 2. There the apostle is referring to the same object to which he is directing the mind of Timothy in the passage now before us, and he says,—"In hope of eternal life, which God, that can not lie, *promised* before the world began," or, "before the times of the ages." And he adds,—"but hath in due time manifested His word through preaching which is committed to me," etc. Now, the " purpose and grace " that are spoken of to Timothy, are here set before us as *promised* before " the times of the ages;" and, if we ask, WHEN was life in Jesus *promised* to men, we can not go back into eternity for the answer. All idea of eternity, and secret decrees, are thus dismissed from the subject. A promise given, is a purpose given, or revealed; and the promise here referred to, as fulfilled by the appearing of Jesus, was a grace indeed, and a grace promised to men. The same subject is spoken of in Romans xvi. 25. There it is said to have been " kept secret " since, or rather "*in*" the times of the ages. The words of the apostle bear, that the proclamation was *silent*, that is, when compared with what it was to be in gospel days. The whole of these allusions of the apostle to " the times of the ages," show us, that he looks to the time when the purpose of God to abolish death, by the death of His Son, was given to mankind in the promise of Jehovah. This leads us at once back to the time when this purpose of the atonement of Jesus was given, at the commencement of the dispensations in the garden of Eden, when God said that the seed of the woman should bruise the head of the serpent. This was God's purpose, and it was His grace too, and it was such given to men; and, though not proclaimed as fully as in gospel days, yet it was no longer kept any secret in His own breast. See, then, my hearer, how clearly the Scriptures expound themselves, when you are prepared to take their own exposition, and how gloriously they cast off, as with almighty energy, the load of predestination and partial purposes, by which they have been burdened by man. They lead you to God in Christ, as giving forth His great design, so that, by resting upon it in prospect, man might be saved, and show you the accomplishment of His purpose, as the still more clear manifestation of His design that man may be called to rest upon the finished work of Jesus, purposed and promised before the times of the ages, but now made manifest by the victorious death of that precious Saviour. O! rejoice that you have such a leader as the Lamb of God. Trust to His teachings as thus placed before you, and you will be made " wise unto salvation."

II. LET US NOW CONSIDER THE BEARING OF THIS PURPOSE AND GRACE UPON MEN UNIVERSALLY.

It is not my intention to enter upon the subject of the "*call*" here spoken of, and regarded by many as an "effectual call," which God purposed from all eternity to give to a certain number of men. It is clear, from what we have already seen, that this call is according to the atonement of Jesus, and not an eternal and partial choice, taking some and leaving others; and this call, if understood as an *invitation*, must be God's invitation to His love, given on the ground of Jesus' death. The great truth now before us, is the *extent* of "the purpose and grace" here spoken of. To whom were they given " before the times of the ages?" Were they given to *some* men or *to all?*

1. *The purpose as first given, embraced, from its very nature*, ALL MEN. The declaration, on

God's part, that it was His purpose to destroy, or to bruise, the head of the tempter, embraced all men. It can not possibly be regarded as of less extent, without absurdity; for how could the head be bruised for one, and yet remain whole for another? Satan, by the sin of man, had gained a deadly power over them, for he had brought down upon them the force of divine justice itself; and, if this deadly power was to be taken from him, it could not be so for one, without being so for all. It is most clear, then, that no man was excluded from that most gracious purpose given to men " before the times of the ages." It was the *magna charta* —the great and gracious *title-deed* of the whole guilty and condemned race of man, given to all. O! it is like the heart of Him who gave it. My hearer, your name is in that blessed deed—YOU were an object of that mighty grace. Yes, you may not believe it,—you may not regard it,—you may "*neglect* so great salvation,"—you may count the purpose and its accomplishment a trifle and a dream—that does not alter the purpose, or change the nature, or contract the wide embrace of its glorious accomplishment. It remains the same. It was Jehovah's purpose to make a full atonement for all men. He has accomplished that purpose, and thus has broken the deadly power of their guilt, and made them free to His eternal love.

2. *The predictions that revived in men's minds the purpose and grace given them, have the same extensive bearing.* "All we like sheep have gone astray—we have turned every one unto his own way, and the Lord hath laid upon Him the iniquity

of us all." Is. liii. 6. This was the purpose bursting forth, as it were, into maturity before the time. It was the *anticipation* of its manifestation, in the spirit of liveliest prophecy. How beautifully it accords with the purpose and grace given at first! There is no narrowing of the wide embrace of the love and perfection of the atonement:—"The iniquities of us ALL." Oh, my hearer! do you not see your part in this most blessed purpose? Do you not see how, by laying your iniquities upon Jesus, the Lord has so effectually removed them from you, that you are as welcome to His love as if you had never sinned? This is the purpose unto which it was the delight of Paul to turn the dying eyes of men—it was the accomplishment of this purpose that constituted the theme of that gospel which he rejoiced to preach at the risk of life itself. Why should you turn your mind away from so glorious an object? Why, especially, should you have it supplanted by that horrid idea of men divided by a fearful decree, and fixed, one part to life and another to eternal death?

3. *The announcement of the appearing of Jesus has the same universal bearing.* "Behold," said the angel that announced His birth, "I bring you good tidings of great joy, which shall be to all people." The tidings were concerning the manifestation of God's "purpose and grace" spoken of in the passage before us. "Unto you is born a Saviour." These were the tidings. They were glad tidings to ALL PEOPLE. They were tidings of the accomplishment so far of the purposes of God. He had now become the seed of the woman, and was prepared

to go forward as the sacrifice to bruise the head of the serpent. Are you not, then, my hearer, among the " ALL PEOPLE?" Surely, this includes you. So, then, does the purpose and grace of your God. And thus we see that it always did include you, inasmuch as it always was the purpose of your God to make full atonement FOR YOU.

4. *John the Baptist's ever-memorable sentence has the same force.* "Behold the Lamb of God bearing the sins of the world!" This was a still more mature manifestation of the "purpose and grace given us in Christ Jesus before the times of the ages." See, then, the blessed fullness of that purpose. See, especially, my hearer, how it embraces you,—"The sins of the world." Are not you a part of "the world?" Your sins, then, were borne by Jesus. Oh, it is impossible you can think too earnestly or deeply on that truth. It is like a mine of inexhaustible wealth, the riches of which are "righteousness and peace, and joy in the Holy Ghost." The more you dig the more you will be enriched by these precious blessings. Instead of the purpose being such that the less you study it the better, it is such that the soul will live upon it for evermore.

5. *I will close this chain of evidence, which might be much extended, by stating the accomplishment of Jehovah's purpose in the words of Paul.* "There is one God and one Mediator between God and men, the man Christ Jesus, who gave Himself a RANSOM FOR ALL." Surely, this shows sufficiently that the purpose is no limited one. The ransom is given, and that for all men. The difference between

this doctrine of the Spirit of God, and that which teaches that the purpose and grace are limited to a few, is sufficiently manifest. Here, then, we have a truth that can not *permit* the doctrine of a limited and contracted purpose to live with it in the same intelligent faith. You must reject either the one or the other; and surely it is not difficult to choose between them. It is choosing between the barren notion of a contracted theology and the sacrifice of Jesus for the world's sins. Would you, then, my hearer, be "called according to the purpose and grace which was given us in Christ Jesus before the world began," you see now how you must be called. You must be so according to the atonement of Jesus. You must become the child of God through faith in the Saviour's perfect propitiation. It was thus that Paul and Timothy were called, and thus alone can any man approach the Lord of Hosts. "Not according to our works"— were we to ask Him to accept of us according to these, our acceptance must be rejection—but according to the atonement of our Lord and Saviour, the guiltiest are welcome to take their place in the family of God, and, looking up in confidence and love, to cry, "Abba! Father!" Now is *your* time, my hearer, if not yet saved and accepted, to be so according to the work of your Redeemer.

LECTURE VIII.

PREDESTINATION AND THE WICKEDNESS OF MEN.

The passage which I wish to introduce to your mind, under this head, is Prov. xvi. 4. In our authorized translation it stands thus:—"The Lord made all things for Himself, yea, even the wicked for the day of evil." As will be seen by the following quotation, already noticed, this passage is supposed to teach the foreordination of the sin and the doom of the reprobate, with great certainty:—"Observe, all things being at God's disposal, and the decision of life and death belonging to Him, He orders all things by His counsel and decree in such a manner, that some men are born from the womb to certain death, that His name may be glorified in their destruction."* Such, then, is the meaning attached to the word of God, which it is now our duty to consider. The language of the expositor is plain enough, and strong enough. He is not one who wishes to have His words misunderstood, or who is afraid of His own doctrine. Let us, then, ask if this is a true exposition of the passage in question.

I. CONSIDER THE CONNECTION IN WHICH THIS TEXT OCCURS.

You are aware, my hearer, that the intention of

* Calvin's Inst., book iii. chap. xxiii.

a writer is to be known especially by the current of thought found in all that he says on a particular topic; and although this text occurs in a list of "proverbs," it has a remarkable connection, both with what goes before and with what follows it.

1. *Mark the verse that goes before:* "Commit thy works unto the Lord, and thy thoughts shall be established." We shall see how appropriately the verse we have more especially in hand is immediately to follow this. When is it that a man has greatest need of committing his works unto the Lord? Is it not when he is surrounded by the wicked? Often times the child of God is so beset, by the cunning and malice of the ungodly, that he sees no way of escaping from the snare in which, to all appearance, he is fatally involved. The enemy of his soul seems to have completed a victory over him; and he stands as if at his wit's end. Here is the time when he requires the exhortation to commit his works to the Lord, with the assurance that his thoughts shall be established. As an example, we may take the case of a man against whom an injurious report has been circulated. It may be, that the lie has been so artfully constructed that it has gained extensive credit; and he has no evidence whatever to prove to others that it is false. For a time, "the wicked" seem to have triumphed, and even the power and wisdom of God seem to have been overreached. Then, in these trying circumstances, the man of uprightness is told to commit "his works unto the Lord," with the assurance that his "thoughts shall be established." So much, then, for the exhortation that precedes this passage.

2. *Observe the verse that goes immediately after the one chiefly before us.* "Every one that is proud in heart is an abomination to the Lord; though hand join in hand he shall not be unpunished." There are two leading truths in this verse—the wicked pride of man is an *abomination* to Jehovah. How, then, we may well ask, could He decree and foreordain that which is an abomination to His own mind? The doctrine we are opposing is fraught with this absurdity, that God Himself decreed the very things that are an abomination to Him. Oh, surpassing folly! Unaccountable wisdom and learning! The wisdom and learning that make men believe that God Himself has foreordained those things that are loathsome to His spirit, now that they have come to pass! But the passage also brings in the idea of the certainty of punishment for those who, after all, are only fulfilling the decrees of God! Mark, my hearer, the connection. The man who is beset by the wicked, and apparently overpowered by them, is not only told that he is to commit his works unto the Lord that his thoughts may be established, but he is told that those who appear to have the victory are an abomination to Jehovah, and will be assuredly punished. This is to the purpose. This is fitted to uphold him who has been surrounded and overpowered by a wicked enemy. But there is more light still. I have shown you the previous verse, and also the following one—there is a needful link between them. The man may be apt to say, or to think if he do not say, that the wicked have risen above God. It is to meet this thought that the words of Wisdom are

used regarding the wicked. It is to remove this temptation that the passage in hand is provided.

II. Consider, then, the meaning of the verse more especially before us.

In order to see this clearly it may be as well to point out some things which it does *not* say, as well as some that it does.

1. *It does not say that God made men wicked.* Unless this were the declaration in the text, it is of no use to prove the predestination of sin. It is an undoubted truth that God made men who make themselves wicked—God made these men that are now wicked just as He made those who are now righteous. But, surely, it is the most unjustifiable perversion of words to say, that because the Scriptures declare that God made wicked men—men who are now wicked, that the Bible traces the fact of their wickedness to God. The Bible does ascribe their creation to Him who is the Creator of all, but never *can* trace their wickedness to Him who is most holy. Mark, then, my hearer, that this text does not say that God made men wicked, but that He made those who are wicked men of their own choice. It is easy to make the distinction between the simple truth and an atrocious error. "Jehovah made the wicked." They are in His hand and under His control.

2. *The passage before us does not say that God made the wicked* FOR *the day of evil.* It is only the translators who say this; and they do so because their minds were previously imbued with the

idea that God had created some men for destruction. "The day of evil" is properly the day of ruin, or of destruction. It is that awful day on which the wicked shall find all their opportunities of change gone, and their doom fixed. To ascribe to God the creation of men FOR this day is most fearful. As if He looked forward from eternity and decreed the scenes of that dreadful time, and (that these might not fail to come) created millions of souls for the very purpose, that they might serve as fuel for the fire of wrath at that dire season! Again I say, the text teaches no such idea as it stands in the original Scriptures. The particle translated "*for*," and which, in the text before us, makes the idea appear of God making men *for* evil, or for ruin, means properly* "*until*." For this rendering we have not only the highest authority, as may be seen from the note below, but also clear instances from the Scriptures themselves. From them it appears clearly that the particle thus used directs attention to the period previous to, and until the time specified. Amos iv. 7: "When there were yet three months *to* (or *until* or previous to) harvest." Here the use of the particle in question is quite clear and decisive. We have another similar instance in Deut. xvi. 4: "Remain *until* morning." Here the particle is translated by the word "until." So far, then, as we have gone the truth is clear. The Lord made all things—He made even the wicked—and He made the wicked so that they occupy a certain position previous to and until the

* Gesenius says of this preposition, "5. Spoken of *time*, it denotes א the point of time *to* or *until* which something is done."

day of destruction. We shall see the force and importance of His saying "until the day of destruction" afterward. Our first duty is to see what position the wicked occupy until that day.

3. *Let us now ascertain the meaning of the words translated "for Himself."* This we will do most satisfactorily by looking to those instances in which the same phrase occurs which is here so translated. The examination conducted on this principle will not be tedious, as the word to be understood occurs in only seven other instances in the Bible. In every one of these it is rendered *differently* from the way in which it is here given. This is remarkable; but our object is to find its true meaning. Job xxxii. 3: "They found no *answer*." The word here rendered "*answer*," is that which occurs in the verse before us, and which is not given in the translation at all. It occurs between the two particles rendered "for himself." It evidently means, in Job, that which was expected to be *spoken*, or the *words* which were expected to be heard. The same is its meaning in the 5th verse of the same chapter: "When Elihu saw that there was no *answer*,"—when he perceived that nothing was said. Here, again, the word clearly means something that is spoken. Prov. xv. 1: "A soft *answer* turneth away wrath." Here, again, the word clearly signifies that which is spoken. In the same chapter, verse 23, it is said, "A man has joy by the *answer* of his mouth." Here, again, it must clearly mean the things that are spoken. Then, in Prov. xvi. 1 it occurs, "The preparations of the heart in man, and the *answer* of the tongue is from the Lord."

Clearly, here again, the word signifies that which is spoken by the tongue. Prov. xxix. 19: "Though he understand he will not *answer*." Here, again, the word signifies that which is spoken: and the clearest instance to our purpose comes last in order. Micah iii. 7: "Then shall the seers be ashamed, and the diviners confounded; yea, they shall all cover their lips; for there is no *answer* of God." Here the word clearly signifies the *spoken word*, or *oracle* of God. Now, take the only remaining instance in which the word occurs, and translate it according to this, its now evident meaning, and how will it stand?—"The Lord hath made all things according to His oracle—yea, even the wicked until the day of destruction." Such is, unquestionably, the meaning of the Spirit of God; and, instead of sending us away to a hidden decree, that we may satisfy ourselves with mysterious ignorance as our consolation, it bids us to look to the word of God and see His ways, and take that courage with which every part of that word aims to inspire the children of Jehovah.

We are now prepared to see the reason why the sacred writer says "*until*," or "previous to the day of destruction." The grand difficulty of the mind, in regard to the wicked, does not respect that position *at* or *after* that final day, but *previous* to it. It is during this period of trial that they often seem to occupy a position inconsistent with the supremacy of justice in the universe. We are, therefore, informed, that even now the position they occupy, previous to that day, is described by the oracle of God, and the description is such, as to remove all fear from him who attends to it, as to the power of the wicked. The Psalmist teaches us the value of this truth. Ps. lxxiii. 12–17: "Behold, these are the ungodly who prosper in the world, they increase in riches. Verily, I have cleansed my heart in vain, and washed my hands in innocency. For all the day long have I been plagued, and chastened every morning. If I say, I will speak thus: behold, I should offend against the generation of thy children. When I thought to know this, it was too painful for me. Until I went into the sanctuary of God; then understood I their end." Here you are told what his temptation was, and how he was freed from its power. He thought, at first, that it was in vain to be righteous, for the wicked were the prosperous. But he went into the sanctuary, and there consulting the word of the Lord, he saw how the wicked had been made and situated by their Creator, and his mind was at rest. The temptation of the Psalmist has been that of millions. Not one who has consulted the word of God as to the real nature of Jehovah's works, even in His creation of the wicked, have failed to have the temptation at once deprived of its power. They have been made to see by that word that, even *previous to* the day of final trial, the position of the wicked, from the nature which God gave them, and the laws under which He has placed them by their creation, is in clear and perfect accordance with both justice and love. Observe, then, my hearer, if your mind is stumbled by the state of the wicked among men, as their state now appears to your mind previous to the day of their final reckoning, your full relief is found where the Psalmist found his mind set at rest —that is, in the oracles of God. There you will see Jehovah cleared from every possible idea that would cast a dark shade over His glory, by making Him appear either as the originator, or as the favorer of iniquity. You will see there the supremacy of truth and righteousness in His great universe— yea, even in the state of the wicked as they now exist on the earth. This shows us fully the meaning of the verse before us, and prepares our way for the application of the truth contained in it. We shall, therefore, endeavor to follow out somewhat the principles to which we are directed by this passage.

III. LET US NOW SEE HOW GOD HAS MADE ALL THINGS, YEA EVEN THE WICKED.

The text with which we are especially concerned, tells us that God has made all things according to His word—not according to any *secret* decree, but according to His mind revealed in His testimony to those He inspired to speak to mankind.

1. *We are informed in the word of God, that He made all things "very good."* His work of creation was such, that His own holy eye rested upon it with infinite delight. It is unnecessary to dwell upon this in our present connection.

2. *We are informed by the Bible, that "the Lord made man upright."* This is the reverse of His making man wicked. It is like the glorious heart and hand of the self-existent One to make a

pure and holy being, such as man was when he sprung from the hand of his Creator.

3. *We are further informed by the Bible, that God made man in His own image.* Jehovah created the immortal spirit of man, so that the creature should bear the likeness of the Creator. One chief feature of Jehovah's character is His liberty—His will, which just signifies His freedom—His true liberty. Man was made, then, with this freedom, as real, though in a limited degree, as that of God Himself. This is most distinctly implied in the Scripture fact, that Jehovah made man to exercise dominion over the other creatures. Where there is no real will or power of *originating* action, there can be no real dominion, any more than there can be any likeness to the moral image of God in a machine driven by some physical power. Freedom, indeed, is essential to the idea of holiness itself. It is in this perfect, though limited liberty of will, that we see the greatness of the love of God in the creation of man. It is the basis, indeed, of all that raises the glory of the creation of man above that of the creation of an inferior creature. It is the highest or essential attribute of man to be free, as it is essential to every other thing in which he can be said to bear the likeness of God. It is in this, too, that Jehovah is vindicated from all share in the sins of men. He made us so that we ourselves are capable of being the *first* causes of our actions. His so making us was essential to the design of His love to make us like Himself; but in making us capable of being the first causes of our own conduct, He necessarily made us capable of causing

that which is wrong—of being wicked. The criminality of sin consists in its being an abuse of the highest gift that God could bestow in our creation. The capability of free holiness is used in every sin, to create a curse instead of a blessing. Thus, according to the word of God, He made man, and, consequently, every wicked man *free*. This, however, would be no consolation to him who requires to commit his works to the Lord that his thoughts may be established, further than as it frees, in his mind, Jehovah from all share in the causing of the wickedness. It is so far a blessed thought—a heart-relieving thought, to those who have been taught to think that God predestinated even the wickedness of the wicked. It is the lifting of an immense burden from the soul, to see that Jehovah created man for holiness and in uprightness, though they have themselves "sought out many inventions." Still, even under this thought, the mind is not fully satisfied; there is a felt want of something more. We can not be at ease, even though we see that God has no part, directly or indirectly, in the wickedness by which we may be injured and oppressed. We must feel that, free as man is, and clear as God is, from all share in his sin, there is an omnipotent control limiting the extent of his freedom, so that it shall not pass beyond certain bounds.

4. *We are, then, informed by the Bible, that Jehovah created man under His own control.* He gave him a law, with a penalty that marked the boundary of his liberty. He thus surrounded him with the circle of his own omnipotence, so that, while perfectly free *within* that circle, he could not

possibly pass beyond it. While Jehovah made man like Himself, He did not (according to the word) set him above Himself, or beyond His own Almighty reach. This was impossible; and the oracles of God most clearly show us the subordination of the really free creature to the supreme Creator. All the statements of the book of God bring out both these ideas, that man is truly free, and that his range is limited by the supreme control of his great Creator. But even this is not all; this does not fill up the desires of the heart of the oppressed, as they anxiously inquire how Jehovah has made the wicked.

5. *The Bible informs us, therefore, that "all things are made to work together for good to those that love God;" and that even "the wrath of man" is made "to praise Him."* This is the truth that leads a man to commit his works to the Lord. It is the fact, that not one wicked deed will be permitted by the great Creator, beyond the line within which they are all overruled for good. "The remainder" of wrath Jehovah restrains. The glory of God is seen in this, that while He has created man capable of free action—capable of doing wrong as well as right, He has so created him that he shall do no more wrong than He can turn to good account. Especially is this the case in regard to the wrong which one man does to another—the oppressor to the oppressed. Man may, and does eternally ruin himself, but he can not do that which it is beyond the skill and power of God to make a blessing in the end to those who may suffer from it severely now. We might bring out many other

points of truth from the " oracle " of God regarding His creation of all things, even of the wicked until the final day. This is manifestly *the* truth in hand in the verse before us; and to this, therefore, I direct all your attention.

In conclusion, then, and in order to illustrate this point more fully, let us suppose the sovereign of a free and happy country. Let us suppose that a band of subjects of that sovereign became traitors. Is this for his honor? Were it supposed that he secretly decreed this treason, in order that he might have an opportunity of condemning it, and executing the men who had become guilty, would not everlasting infamy cleave to his name? But suppose that he has no such decree, and that his most secret heart is set upon the good of all his subjects. These traitors introduce their iniquity purely of their own accord, and against every feeling and design of the sovereign. Suppose that he is so wise and so mighty, that he is perfectly able to bring a vast amount of good out of this evil: this is truly glorifying to him. Such is the case with God: He has created all things—all men,—those who are wicked, as well as those who are righteous, with a view to the universal good; and so that, even those who dishonor Him, and bring in treason into the universe, shall not go beyond Him, but shall be made, in defiance of their uncaused transgression and malice, to contribute individually to the great aim—" *unti*" the day of destruction." This is the very truth required by those who are called upon to commit their works to the Lord, with the assurance that their thoughts shall be established. Oh! my hear-

or, it may be that you have been surrounded by the wicked—you may be in difficulty because of the oppressor—you may be surrounded as by a wall of iron by the efforts of malice—you may be ready to feel as if the wicked had outdone Jehovah—it may be impossible for you to see how you can have confidence, seeing the guilty triumph. Here, then, is your rest—even the wicked are so formed, that they are within the circle drawn by Him whose heart is love. Peacefully commit your course to Him: be assured that He will bring your feet out of the net. The worst men that ever lived have only been created capable of a limited degree of wrong; and He who made them—gave them their freedom, and at the same time assigned them their limits—has them fully under His control; so that, out of all their evil He can still evolve the good. Know this truth fully—view it in the light of the glory of God as it shines in the face of Jesus, and you will be glad in the Lord, with exceeding joy.

LECTURE IX.

PREDESTINATION AND THE STUMBLING OF MEN.

The text to which I now turn your attention is 1 Peter, ii. 8, where Jesus is said to to be "a stone of stumbling, and rock of offense, even to them which stumble at the word, being disobedient; *whereunto also they were appointed.*" The doctrine of reprobation is supposed to be very distinctly taught in this passage. One of the mildest and best of authors has the following comment on the words: "'Whereunto, also, they were appointed.' This, the apostle adds," he says, "for the further satisfaction of believers on this point, how it is that so many reject Christ and stumble at Him; telling them plainly, that the secret purpose of God is accomplished in this: God having determined to glorify His justice on impenitent sinners, as He shows His mercy in them that believe." It is not without some reason that this honest writer immediately adds,—"Here it were easier to lead you into a deep, than to lead you forth again." * His idea is, that their stumbling at the word is the result of God's appointment. Let us, then, consider whether this is truth or error.

* Leighton on Peter's Epistles.

I. Consider some objections that may be urged against this idea of the passage.

By a calm consideration of these, the mind may be led more earnestly to inquire into the real meaning of the text.

1. *To suppose that this " stumbling " was the accomplishment of God's appointment, is contrary to the approval of faith, and the condemnation of unbelief, on the part of the Apostle.* He is describing, in one part of his epistle, the judgment or dreadful calamity that was coming on the generation in which he lived; and he says,—" For the time is come that judgment must begin at the house of God; and, if it first begin at us, what shall the end be of them that *obey not the gospel of God?* " Now, were the idea before us correct, the disobedient are as truly accomplishing the will —the *real will* of God as the righteous; and no man can help getting into a " *deep*," if he hold that the wicked are to be punished for that which God both willed and appointed. He will get into a deep, from which he will not only be unable to lead others forth, but from which he will not soon come forth himself. The exposition that so involves even the expositor, should be most suspiciously canvassed. Every man of common sense will *think* ere he accept it.

2. *The idea of the " stumbling " being appointed of God is contrary to all God's expressions in regard to sin.* His true character is given in these words,—" Thou art of purer eyes than to behold evil, and canst not look upon sin." But stumbling

at the word is the most deadly of all sins; and the doctrine before us is, that He could not only look upon it, but that He could see in it the accomplishment of His own secret purpose! There is depth and height here, but it is the depth of error and the height of folly. We can not but feel convinced that there must be something sadly wrong with an exposition that represents the worst of sins as the accomplishment of the secret purpose of a sin-hating God. My hearer, are you fully satisfied in your mind that Jewish rejection of the gospel—the vilest of all sins, was actually the accomplishment of the purpose of Him who "*can not look upon sin?*" Are you not constrained to think there must be error here?

3. *The idea before us is directly opposed to the Bible doctrine, that sin is not an honor, but a dishonor to God.* "Through breaking the law *dishonorest* thou God." This is Paul's doctrine. And while it is true that God vindicates His character in punishing sin, it is not true that sin or unbelief contributes to His honor as an appointment of His. All the honor that could be conceived of as arising from His punishment of sin, would be extinguished the moment it is admitted that He is only punishing that which He had appointed Himself. This, then, is another most serious and fatal objection to the exposition now under our consideration. Sin can only be seen to honor God in the infinite opposition with which He regards it.

4. *The most fatal objection, however, is that such an exposition is entirely uncalled for, even by the very exceptionable translation of the text*

given in our common version. There is no reason why the word "appointed" should apply to the "stumbling" or to the "disobedience," rather than to "the word." The Jews were appointed to hear the word of God: and if a man were not under the influence of very strong prejudice indeed, he would see that they were appointed to the word, and never would he dream that they were appointed to stumble and disobey! Before any one can be justified in deriving such a fearful doctrine from the word of God, the doctrine must be there; but before even such exposition can be palliated, it must be shown that the expositor is *shut up* to the idea. All that is needed to show, that instead of the stumbling of the Jews being of God's appointment, it was *against* His appointment, is to direct the "appointed" to "the word," instead of referring it to the sin.

It will not be a matter of wonder, then, if, on these grounds, the exposition before us be totally rejected. O! let the hearer rejoice that it can be rejected; for of all the calamities that could fall upon the universe, this would be the most dreadful—to have a God who could secretly appoint the stumbling and disobedience of men, and then punish them for carrying out His own decree. We shall see, and that from this very passage, how gloriously different is the character and secret heart of Jehovah.

II. LET US NOW CONSIDER THE BIBLE TRUTH THAT IS TAUGHT IN THIS PASSAGE.

It is a blessed thing not only to remove the error, but also to evolve the truth—not only to pull down, but also to build up.

1. *What is* "THE WORD" *here spoken of?* There is very great importance in this question. It is important, not only from the striking light in which it sets the whole subject, but also from the striking manner in which the answer is found in this epistle itself. In the first chapter, from the 23d to the 25th verse, we have this striking description of this word: "Being born again, not of corruptible seed, but of incorruptible, by THE WORD of God, which liveth and abideth forever. For all flesh is grass, and all the glory of man as the flower of grass: the grass withereth, and the flower thereof falleth away; but the word of the Lord endureth forever. And this is THE WORD which, by the gospel, is preached unto you." Here there can be no room for doubt as to what the word is at which the disobedient stumbled. It was the gospel —the very gospel by which the believers had been born again—the glad tidings that Jesus had died for their sins. They *stumbled* at this! Most astonishing and most guilty stumbling! The greatest revelation of love the universe ever saw—the most perfect display of excellence that created intelligence could be called to contemplate—this was their stumbling-stone and rock of offense! No crime could be greater—no depth of base ingratitude and malignity could be more fearful; and how is it possible for the soul of man to entertain the thought, that this base and most abominable malignity was appointed of God? Only think of the love and loveliness of Jesus,—only remember that

the light of the glory of God shone in His face,—only remember that this same Jesus was "AN OFFENSE" to these men; and then hear that THIS was the accomplishment of the secret appointment of God! But we must proceed.

2. *Consider the nature of the "stumbling" spoken of here.* The word "stumbling" is apt to convey to our minds the idea of something blind, and deaf, and stupid, rather than something *wicked*. It is much more clearly rendered,—"who are offended by the word." The word was an offense—a hated object,—that at which they were ready to put on an expression of malignant contempt when it was preached to them. The idea is not that of a man stumbling over some object that lies in his way in the dark, but that of being offended and irritated—enraged at an object which is obtruded on the notice of him who is offended. Such is the sin which, it is supposed, was a secret appointment of God. Alas! poor humanity! how fearful must be that darkness that permits the entrance of such a thought! How far astray the ideas of God that can ever permit it to have a place among them!

3. *Consider further the expressed cause of their stumbling, or taking offense.* The words of Peter are as follows:—"These being *unpersuaded* [or rather, if I may use the word, *unpersuadable*] take offense," etc. The disobedience is that of the unbeliever who has a plain, simple, and glorious truth, with most powerful evidence, pressed upon his mind by the Spirit of God, and remains still unpersuaded. He is *unpersuadable.* This was the real case of the unbelieving Jews, and also of the

Gentiles, who took offense at the word of the gospel of Jesus. The apostles had to turn from them, because they put the word of God away from their minds, and would not be persuaded. They always resisted the Spirit of God. This state of mind was the cause, the free, voluntary cause of their stumbling, or taking offense at the gospel. Surely, if there is one state of mind more detestable to God than another, it is that in which all the motives contained in the *love,* and *tears,* and *blood* of Jesus, are urged upon a man by the Spirit, and yet he remains unmoved. And yet we are taught to believe that this state of mind is appointed of God! No, my hearer, we reject the imputation, and would not for ten thousand worlds harbor the suspicion that is so ruinous to enlightened confidence in Jehovah.

4. *Consider the nature of the appointment that is mentioned in the text before us.* The word which is translated "appointed," here, *never* has the meaning of a secret fore-appointment of anything. Its literal meaning is that of *placing* or *setting* an object in a particular situation, and it refers to the actual placing, never to the intention or determination to place. The verse ought, therefore, to be rendered thus:—"These being unpersuadable, take offense at the word into which even they were placed." The idea is perfectly clear,—they were placed by God in the very midst of gospel light. It shone around them; it enveloped them in an atmosphere of truth and love; and, just because they were placed in the very midst of the rays of the Sun of Righteousness, they were irritated to a

deadly degree at that very light. Here, then, we see, that instead of appointing them to take offense, Jehovah placed them in the best conceivable position for seeing His true character, and being His children for ever. O! how wide the contrast between these two doctrines! God secretly determining that these men should hate the truth, that He might "glorify" His justice in their punishment; and God taking inveterate rebels and placing them in the very center of the beams of His concentrated glory of justice and love, that they might be saved! To which of these, my hearer, does your heart turn, as to the God of its choice? Surely, there is no great difficulty in deciding. If you think that I draw too dark a picture of the doctrine I am now opposing, then read it in the words of its own advocates—read it in the words which I have already quoted. Bring these side by side with the text now under consideration, and make your choice. But, above all, remember that this subject comes home to your own case. *You are placed in the Word* as were the Jews and Gentiles of old. The love and justice of your God have been presented to you, as they appear in the wounds and agonies of a crucified Jesus. You know how you have felt to this object. You know if you have rather wished to think seldom of Him, and have indulged the tendencies that lead the soul to dwell upon any object in preference to Jesus. O! let me, in deep earnest, beseech you to turn to Him. Let Him be your chief study—your great delight. Believe Him to be what He is, and He will be "precious" to your soul. O! let that spirit which God has ransomed, by the offering of His Son, be not only filled with the riches of His grace; but let it be the means of promoting widely the enjoyment of these by your fellow-men, who all around you are perishing for lack of knowledge.

LECTURE X.

PREDESTINATION AND THE INFATUATION OF THE REPROBATE.

THERE are a considerable number of passages in which it is supposed that God teaches the doctrine of His blinding and stupefying men. These are chiefly, however, quotations, or allusions, belonging to that text found in Isaiah vi. 9–12; and we shall consider the greater part of them in this lecture, under that passage of the prophet. It is as follows, —"And He said, Go and tell this people, Hear ye indeed, but understand not; and see ye indeed, but perceive not. Make the heart of this people fat, and make their ears heavy, and shut their eyes; lest they see with their eyes, and hear with their ears, and understand with their heart, and convert, and be healed. Then said I, Lord, how long? And He said, Until the city be wasted without inhabitant, and the houses without man, and the land be utterly desolate, and the Lord have removed men far away, and there be a great forsaking in the midst of the land." Such is the translation given of the words of Jehovah to the "evangelical prophet;" and the utmost use has been made of these to deepen, if possible, the darkest shades of the doctrine of reprobation. The great Calvin speaks of them as follows:—"But the mission of Isaiah furnishes a still stronger confirmation; for this is his mission from the Lord,—'Go and tell this people, Hear ye indeed,'" etc. "Observe," says Calvin, "He directs His voice to them, but it is that they may become more deaf; He kindles a light, but it is that they may be made more blind; He publishes His doctrine, but it is that they may be more besotted; He applies a remedy, but it is that they may not be healed." This is a part of the proof of a statement given a little before, where he says,—"It is a fact, not to be doubted, that God sends His word to many, whose blindless He determines shall be increased." Such, then, is the melancholy picture of Jehovah's character, which is derived from this passage of His word; and, surely, no duty can be much more binding upon us, than to search most diligently the foundations of such a doctrine, lest we be found guilty of libeling our great Creator, by misunderstanding and misinterpreting His word. In order that this search may be felt to be deeply needful, I shall first state some of the difficulties that lie in the way of our receiving this doctrine of Calvin.

I. CONSIDER SOME MANIFEST OBJECTIONS THAT LIE AGAINST THE DOCTRINE NOW STATED.

The mind will appreciate the right interpretation of the passage, in proportion as it realizes the real nature of that doctrine which is given in the words of Calvin.

1. *The doctrine in question is contrary to Bible views of God's hatred of sin.* The blindness, which is said to be increased by the determination

of God, is *sinful* blindness. So is the stupidity and obduracy of heart said to be increased by the same determination. These are not only sin, but, as we have already said of taking offense at the word, sin of the deepest dye—confessedly the fruitful parent of all other sin. Now, seeing that Jehovah is a God " of purer eyes than to behold evil, and that He can not look upon sin," is it not something strange, and fearfully contradictory, when we are told that He sends a prophet to a people for the very purpose of increasing that sin which He so much abhors? My hearer, have you *no* difficulty in believing, first, that God's infinite mind is filled with loathing toward iniquity, and then believing that He appoints and sends a prophet for the sole purpose of increasing that which constitutes the root and perfection of all wickedness? Do you find no need of an interpretation of the book of God, that shall be more consistent with itself? Would it not be better to say, "I do not understand it," than to understand thus? These questions *must* go home to the heart of every reflecting man, who feels sufficiently the value of the character of God.

2. *The doctrine in question is contrary to every scriptural idea of the striving of the Spirit of God.* Let us see what truth Stephen teaches on this subject. Acts vii. 51, 52,—" Ye stiff-necked and uncircumcised in heart and ears, ye do always resist the Holy Ghost: as your fathers did, so do ye. Which of the prophets have not your fathers persecuted? and they have slain them which showed before of the coming of the Just One; of whom

ye have now been the betrayers and murderers." Here we see the true position of the Spirit of God and His prophets; and, likewise, that of the inveterate depravity of the Jews. That depravity is on one side—God is on the other. The wicked hardness of men is urging one way; God, by His prophets, is striving to turn this accursed tide. This is the true position of God, and of the blindness and obduracy of men. How, then, does this agree with the doctrine that God sent His prophet, and determined that by his mission the obduracy and besotted stupidity of the Jews should be increased? Is it possible, my hearer, for you to believe that God can at the same time be striving to turn the current of wickedness, and also determining that it shall run with still greater force? Can He send a prophet whose mission shall be both to strive to stay the course of sin, and, at the same time, and with the same people, to increase the force of iniquity? Now, you must either believe that the Spirit of God strives against sin, and yet determines its increase, or you must have some other exposition of this text than that which is given by Calvin. That exposition is not only a libel on God, but it bears absurdity on its very forehead. No wonder, when such things are to be credited, that men hold that we are unable to believe without supernatural aid! But where is the aid to come from, by which we are to believe that God strives against sin and for sin at the same time, and with the same persons?

3. *The doctrine before us ascribes the work of the devil to God.* Hear Paul's account of the work of Satan. 2 Cor. iv. 3, 4,—" But if our gospel be

hid, it is hid to them that are lost: in whom the god of this world hath blinded the minds of them which believe not, lest the light of the glorious gospel of Christ, who is the image of God, should shine unto them." Here, then, most clearly, is the work of Satan. It is to blind the minds of unbelievers, lest they should see the gospel. But this is the very work ascribed to God by the doctrine before us! Are we, then, to understand that God and Satan have the same work, and that both are determined to increase the blindness and hardness of the eternally reprobated sinner? Is not the statement of such a monstrous absurdity sufficient for its rejection, by every sober mind? Observe, then, if you do reject it, you must also reject the translation of the verse in hand, and with it the exposition of the verse which we have quoted: and you must also reject the whole of the doctrine, in every phase of it, that represents it as the will and pleasure of God, that sin should be either increased or continued. We have thus stated our objections to the doctrine which is founded upon the translation before us, and these objections will be seen to lie in all their force against the translation itself. We must not, however, fail to mark other objections that lie against the *translation*, and that would be sufficient to prove it erroneous, even were there no false doctrine involved.

II. CONSIDER, THEN, SOME OBJECTIONS THAT LIE AGAINST THE TRANSLATION BEFORE US, SIMPLY CONSIDERED AS A TRANSLATION.

All that has yet been said, can not warrant us to

reject the translation in question. The objections considered, do warrant us in *suspecting* the rendering, but not in rejecting it. Let us be glad, then, that the God of Providence has taken care that we should not want full and convincing evidence that the words of the prophet, and of God, have been fearfully misrepresented.

1. *The* ORIGINAL HEBREW ITSELF, *does not* REQUIRE *the translation given.* The Hebrew of the Bible, was originally written without the points generally known as "the vowel points." These are small signs, written either above or below the line of the original language, intended to guide in the pronunciation of the words, and though not affecting the sense in many cases, they do materially affect it in others. Take these points away, and the language of the prophet is capable of two renderings—either an imperative, or an indicative rendering. Their simple meaning, rendered in the indicative mood, instead of the imperative (and read literally), is, "Hear ye to hear, and ye shall not understand; and see ye to see, and ye shall not perceive. This people have made fat their heart—and they have made heavy their ears—and they have covered their eyes—that they might not see with their eyes, and hear with their ears, and understand with their heart, and turn, and be cured." Such is the plain and most obvious translation of Isaiah's words. So far as the bare words of the prophet are concerned, we are left to choose between these two renderings, the imperative or the indicative, and the connection is more than sufficient to determine which we should take. You see, then, the

true position of the passage, as it came from the hand of the prophet. There is no such fearful doctrine as that we are considering at all contained in it, when it is allowed to speak in its connection, without the aid of the points, which are but a human invention, and that of a date many centuries later than the words of the prophet.* But this does not by any means exhaust the objections to the translation before us. It is not only given in the face of the doctrinal objections noticed, and that, when the words of the prophet require no such translation, but we shall see that it is given in the face of far higher than human authority.

2. *What is generally called the Septuagint version, is against the translation before us.* Although great weight is not to be attached to the Septuagint in some parts, we shall yet see that the *greatest* weight is to be given to it in this. It is a translation of a date at least three centuries earlier than that of the "points," which give the meaning, now under consideration, to the words of the prophet. Had these "points" been in use, and recognized as of any authority, we can not conceive of the translator of Isaiah into Greek, as giving the rendering that has been given. I mention this fact, in order to show the hearer the very *slender* character upon which Calvin rests that most fearful doctrine we have quoted. The prophet's own words do not re-

---

* Gesenius says:—"Of the date of this invention (of the points) we have no account; but a comparison of historical facts warrants the conclusion, that the vowel system was not completed till after the seventh century of the Christian era."— See *Heb. Gram.* p. 14.

quire it; and the *earliest* translation, which we know to have been made of them, rejects it, and ascribes to the people themselves, that which Calvin ascribes to God. We are just advancing to the point at which we shall see that the most hateful libel has been cast upon the character of God, as if on his own authority, when all the authority existing for it, is that of the blundering men who set the points to the Hebrew letters about two hundred and eighty years after the time that Jesus was upon the earth.

3. *The Saviour Himself quotes the words of Isaiah in a way that for ever sets aside the translation before us.* We have His words in Mathew's gospel, xiii. 14, 15:—"And in them is fulfilled the prophecy of Esaias, which saith, By hearing ye shall hear, and shall not understand: and seeing ye shall see, and shall not perceive: for this people's heart is waxed gross, and their ears are dull of hearing, and their eyes they have closed; lest at any time they should see with their eyes, and hear with their ears, and should understand with their heart, and should be converted, and I should heal them." The whole weight of the authority of Jesus is, therefore, brought against the translation upon which the doctrine now before us rests. The Septuagint translation of Isaiah is not, in many things, to be depended on; but as if to meet this most important deficiency in the testimony, the Lord of glory adds His own word of eternal truth to it, and thus confirms the translation of the Septuagint. Well, then, my hearer, what are we to make of the rendering before us? It deeply dis-

honors God—it misleads the soul as to His true character—it represents Him as at one with Satan in blinding the minds of those who believe not—its slender authority is that of the men who "*pointed*" the prophet's language—and it is rejected by the translation of the Septuagint, and, what is infinitely more, by the Saviour Himself. What are we to make of the translation, and of the doctrine founded on it? They perish at once before the majesty of truth, and of the God of truth; and oh, how blessed is it to see them die together! It is indeed like the clearing away of the dense thundercloud, and the shining forth of the morning sun.

4. *But we have yet further authority against the men on whose false gloss the translation in question depends.* Paul quotes the Septuagint version of Isaiah, and thus confirms it by the authority of his inspiration. Acts xxviii. 25–27, "And when they agreed not among themselves, they departed, after that Paul had spoken one word, Well spake the Holy Ghost by Esaias, the prophet, unto our fathers, saying, Go unto this people, and say, Hearing ye shall hear, and shall not understand; and seeing ye shall see, and not perceive: for the heart of this people is waxed gross, and their ears are dull of hearing, and their eyes have they closed; lest they should see with their eyes, and hear with their ears, and understand with their heart, and should be converted, and I should heal them." Here, once more, the blinding and hardening of the soul are ascribed to man himself, and not to God, or the prophet, as in the translation before us. Let the hearer, then, calmly consider this part of the

THE INFATUATION OF THE REPROBATE. 161

subject, and then try how much place the translation before us can have in his mind. You may not be able to read the Hebrew words of Isaiah, or the Greek words of the Septuagint—you are able to read the quotations of them by Jesus and by Paul, and with these you are more than furnished for weighing the rendering under consideration, and finding it fearfully wanting.

5. *Where, then, rests this said undoubted and not to be disputed fact, "that God sends His word to those whose blindness He determines shall be increased?"* We answer, upon the slender and *condemned* authority of those who *pointed* the Hebrew language. Horne, in his invaluable Introduction to the Critical Study of the Scriptures, sets this authority in the clearest light. He says, in a note on this text as quoted in Matt. xiii. 14, 15:—"This quotation is taken almost verbatim from the Septuagint. . . . . In the Hebrew the sense is obscured by FALSE pointing. If, instead of reading it in the imperative mood, we read it in the indicative mood, the sense will be, '*Ye shall hear but not understand:* and *ye shall see but not perceive.* This people hath made their heart fat, and hath made their ears heavy, and shut their eyes,' etc., which agrees in sense with the Evangelist and with the Septuagint, as well as with the SYRIAC and ARABIC versions, but not with the Latin Vulgate. We have the same quotation, word for word, in Acts xxviii. 26. Mark and Luke refer to the same prophecy, but quote it only in part." Horne gives this as a quotation from Dr. Randolph, and thus sets the whole subject distinctly before us. Of the

14*

false points he says, in another place, when setting the arguments for and against their antiquity before the reader, "The weight of evidence, we apprehend, will be found to determine *against* them." Such, then, is the slender, and, I should say, *wretched ground*, on which is rested one of the most fearful doctrines that ever polluted the mind of man, or hid the glories of the God of love. Such is the ground upon which Calvin declares this doctrine to be a *fact* not to be doubted; for although he refers to several other instances, he holds this to be the strongest confirmation of this said "fact." My hearer, is it not time that we were thinking for ourselves in matters that affect our souls and the honor of our God? And if we do think for ourselves at all, and take the undoubted word of God as the ground for our thoughts, must we not reject with abhorrence the doctrine in question, and seek, as God may enable us, to open the eyes of other men to its flimsy and most false character? May we not bless Him who has put it within our reach to study the Bible for ourselves?

III. Consider now some of these passages that consist of quotations of this which has been chiefly under notice in this lecture.

By the view which we are now enabled to take of the parent stem of the several partial quotations, or allusions that occur in the New Testament connected with Isaiah vi. 9, 10, we shall be much more easily able to understand all the branches. We have already seen and considered that of the Saviour in Matthew xiii. 14, 15, and, therefore, need not return to it. Indeed, it is so clear, that it seems quite unnecessary to do any more than allow it to speak for itself. We shall also see the reason why Jesus made the quotation, in considering the same historical facts in other places. We have also considered Paul's quotation of the words of the prophet, and do not require to recur to that. He had done the utmost to lead them to accept of life; and when all seemed hopeless, he warned them, in the words of their own Isaiah, and showed them the dangerous position which they occupied, as he turned with the gospel to the Gentiles. We shall, therefore, turn our minds to the other passages connected with the main subject before us.

1. *Let us look to the words of Jesus as recorded in Luke* viii. 10. "And He said, unto you it is given to know the mysteries of the kingdom of God, but to others in parables; that seeing, they might not see, and hearing, they might not understand." This was the reason which Jesus gave His disciples for speaking to the general multitude in a parable. So far as it is a quotation of Isaiah, it is most important to mark that it is a quotation of the *fact* of their hearing without understanding, and not of the *cause* assigned for that fact. The Saviour declares that He spake to the multitude, and the result was, that hearing they did not understand; but Luke does not give the history so fully as Matthew, and thus we have to recur to the statement in the former gospel for the full truth in that before us. Why, then, did Jesus require to speak

"*so that*," * the great mass of His hearers did not understand? Because they had made their hearts *insensible*, and their ears heavy, and had shut their eyes determinately against the light. They burned with thirst for the blood of Jesus and of His disciples when He brought out the truth without any covering of parable. He took the best possible method of instructing them so as to awaken their *consciences* without rousing their deadly prejudice. He spake to them so that every right heart there would understand Him—so that those who took time and care to reflect on what He said would be moved and benefited, and yet the prejudices of no one would be unnecessarily wounded.† But why did He require this great precaution?—Because of the state in which the people kept their own minds. Take the two parts of the truth together, and you will see that, instead of Jesus speaking *with the design of stupefying His hearers*, He was compelled to speak in the very way He adopted, because they themselves had made their souls unfit for plainer teaching. They had so demonized their spirits that it had become unsafe to warn them of the danger of being unfruitful hearers in anything but the language of parable. Here, again, the love of Jesus shines forth with peculiar luster, and His character is cleared from the foul stain of

---

* The particle rendered "*that*," and appearing to mean "*in order that*," does not necessarily mean so. It very frequently means "*so that*," as well as "*in order that*," and ought to be so understood here.

† Barnes takes the same view. See his Notes on Matthew xiii. 14, 15.

intending to keep the truth from His hearers. He is seen to be so desirous to teach them that He ventures, upon the peril of His life, and that of all who adhere to Him, to teach them, when He can do it only in this distant way. Mark, too, my hearer, that these very men had the warning of Isaiah in their hands; and when they heard without understanding, and saw without perceiving, they might have been alarmed at their own state of heart, and thus been turned from such a dreadful condition of soul. The warning of the prophet—its fulfillment in their experience, and the nature of the Saviour's teaching—all combined to fix their attention upon the fearful crime of which they were guilty—all brought up before them the dread evil of having shut their eyes, and ears, and hearts against the truth of God. How different is all this from the monstrous notion that is expressed in the following words,—" Nor can it be disputed, that to such persons as God determines not to enlighten He delivers His doctrine in enigmatical obscurity, that its only effect may be to increase their stupidity. For Christ testifies that He confined to His disciples the explanation of the parables in which He had addressed the multitude."* On one hand is the merciful and tender-hearted Saviour, on the other a fearful idol of man's creation. Oh, my hearer! well may we be glad, and rejoice, and give praise, that the God of the Bible is not the God who is set forth in the doctrines of universal predestination— well may we prize the Bible that enables us to reject that fearful misrepresentation of Jehovah.

* Calvin's Inst., book iii. chap. xxiv.

2. *Let us consider the account given by John of another fulfillment of Isaiah.* It is found in John xii. 37-41 :—" But though He had done so many miracles before them, yet they believed not on Him : that the saying of Esaias, the prophet, might be fulfilled, which he spake, Lord, who hath believed our report? and to whom hath the arm of the Lord been revealed? Therefore, they could not believe, because Esaias said again, He hath blinded their eyes, and hardened their heart; that they should not see with their eyes, nor understand with their heart, and be converted, and I should heal them. These things said Esaias, when he saw His glory, and spake of Him." Calvin says of this passage : "John, citing this prophecy (of Isaiah), declares that the Jews could not believe because this curse of God was upon them." This is predestination, rank and ripened to its utmost. Mark, then, my hearer, that John quotes a different portion of Isaiah's words from that recorded by Luke. John speaks of the *reason* why the Jews could not believe; and gives the state of their hearts as that reason. Luke speaks of the effect which this state of heart had upon the Saviour's teaching. In both cases, however, it is the state of mind in which the Jews were that is said and seen to be at the foundation of all the evil. In this case, the translation perverts the original. There is no word for "*he*" in the Greek, and we are left to learn from the words quoted elsewhere who blinded their eyes and hardened their heart. We are bound to say who this is from the passage of which this is a partial quotation, or rather of which this is the sub-

stance. In that, the agent blinding is not "he" or "Jesus," but "*this people*." "They could not believe, because, as Isaiah said, *This people* have blinded their eyes and hardened their hearts." Nothing is more melancholy than to see mistranslations that *slander* the Saviour. This is most surely one: and when you take it in its simple and manifest sense it leads you to the free choice of a wicked people, as the only reason why the prediction was fulfilled in their case,—"Who hath belived our report?" Their unbelief was not because of Isaiah's prophecy, but it was the fact that, in their unbelief, that prophecy was verified. Here, again, Jehovah is cleared; and the root and maintenance of iniquity are found in man *alone*. What a fearful idea that all the miracles of Jesus were wrought to harden one set of men and save another! Here we see that infamous error completely set aside; and we are warned against the fatal sin of shutting our eyes upon the truth. "To-day, if ye will hear His voce, harden not your hearts." This is all "*like God*," and when Scripture is permitted thus to explain Scripture, it is like star to star in the firmament, adding their mutual rays, and swelling the general glory of the testimony of God.

3. *Let us, then, consider one of the most apparently difficult passages in that class now especially before us.* Mark iv. 10-12:—" And when He was alone, they that were about Him, with the twelve, asked of Him the parable. And He said unto them, Unto you it is given to know the mystery of the kingdom of God: but unto them that are without, all these things are done in parables. That

seeing they may see, and not perceive; and hearing they may hear and not understand; lest at any time they should be converted, and their sins should be forgiven them." This, as it appears at first sight, is the strongest statement that could be conceived in favor of the doctrine that *God blinds* the minds of men. It also states that He does blind them, "*lest*" they should be converted and forgiven. It favors, nay appears to demonstrate the doctrine, that His desire is to *prevent* the reprobate from enjoying His mercy. The light in which it sets the doctrine is only *too strong*. It forces us to suspect that something must be wrong in the manner in which it is stated, or in which the statement of it is understood. In order to understand it correctly, two things must be especially kept in view.

(1.) Mark is only giving the Saviour's words in part. This is most manifest when we compare his statement with that of Matthew. Mark is giving (as Luke and John do) simply the *substance* of what the Saviour said; hence he leaves out the *reason* why those who were "without" did not *know* and *understand* that which was stated to them in parables. The reason, as given by Matthew, was, that they had shut their eyes, and ears, and heart, *lest* they should be converted. There can not be any room to doubt that this *reason* was in the mind of Mark, as he wrote the verse; but he considered the sentiment expressed fully enough without its formal statement. We shall see reason for this immediately, but at present it is most important to make sure the fact that this reason must be supplied in order to the right understanding of the words of

Jesus. There can be no doubt that Isaiah gave that reason, and laid the sin of their blindness at the door of the Jews themselves. There can be no doubt that Jesus quoted Isaiah on this occasion, and quoted this reason with the rest of the passage; and as there can be no doubt that Mark *intended* to give the full meaning of Jesus' words, he must have considered the state of the heart of the Jews as *implied* in the words which he gave as in substance those of Jesus. This leads us to understand the passage before us, with the implied addition of the reason of Jewish infatuation in it; and we are brought to inquire on what principle Mark could regard it as implied. Implied it must have been; the question arises, how could it be so, seeing no part of it is stated?

(2.) Mark must have regarded Jewish blindness as *voluntary* blindness. He could not but do this; for he had heard Jesus say, that *they had closed their eyes*, lest they should see and be turned. They were declared by Jesus to be willfully blind, and to be *willing* their own blindness, lest He should succeed in their conversion. This points out to us a most important matter in the passage under consideration, and one on which the right understanding of it greatly turns. That is,—to what does the "*lest*" belong? Is it that JESUS so taught them lest they should be converted and forgiven; or, is it that THEY shut their eyes, and would not see, lest they should be converted and forgiven? This is just the question: Was it Jesus or themselves that strove against their conversion? As the passage stands, at first sight, it would appear as if Jesus opposed their conversion; but when you take into account the truly *voluntary* nature of their blindness and obduracy, and the fact that they required, as it were, to *squeeze* their eyes together to keep out the light of truth, the passage represents *them* as blind lest they should be converted and forgiven. They would not, and did not see, lest they should be forgiven. No man, therefore, can use this passage as a proof that Jesus sought to prevent the conversion of men, without setting one part of the Bible against another, and that without the slightest warrant. Because, when to take into account what was involved in their seeing without knowing, and hearing without understanding, viz., the *will* that refused to know and understand, this text speaks the very same truth as those do that give a more full statement of the occurrence which is here only partially recorded.

We have thus fully considered this most important subject of the blinding and stupefaction of those who are supposed to be predestinated from eternity to be destroyed. We have seen the great testimony of God Himself on the subject; and all that comes out of that testimony is, that men harden their hearts, stop their ears, and shut their eyes, lest His gracious desire for their conversion should be gratified. "God is love," is once more clearly expounded and illustrated; and as love, He is once more seen in love's position striving to win souls. That man is depraved, is again proven; and he is seen in a position corresponding to his depravity, opposing the strivings of the kind Spirit of the Lord. O! my hearer, let us rejoice that we have such a Father, and that He has given us the high privilege of studying the Bible for ourselves. Let us not forget our deep and most weighty responsibility, for to whom much is given, from them much shall be rightly required. Let us be fully alive to the love of our God; and lean our souls on His faithful compassion, through the atonement of Jesus. There let us enjoy, and most ardently improve the blessedness of the Sun of Righteousness, and reflect those rays on all around us.

LECTURE XI.

PREDESTINATION AND THE HARDENING OF HEARTS.

The subject which comes under our notice, more especially in this lecture, is the dealings of God with the Egyptians. The history of these, has long been regarded as undeniable proof that God has reprobated from eternity a certain part of mankind, and that He carries out His reprobating decree, by making His providence prove "the savor of death unto death" to such, while it is "the savor of life unto life" unto others. I shall follow out the examination of this part of our subject in connection with Psalm cv. 25—("He turned their hearts to hate His people, and to deal subtly with His servants"); and also, in view of the whole narrative of Jehovah's dealings with the Pharaohs and their subjects, contained in the commencing chapters of the book of Exodus, and alluded to in the ninth chapter of the epistle to the Romans. At the outset, as in other lectures, it may be well that I should state the opinions that have been entertained of those Scriptures, in the words of those who have published the doctrine of universal predestination as founded on them. The following quotations set the doctrine before us as clearly and fully as could be desired :—" With respect to His secret influences, the declaration of Solomon concerning the heart of a king, that it is inclined hither or thither, according to the divine will, certainly extends to the whole human race, as though he had said, that whatever conceptions we form in our minds, they are directed by the secret inspiration of God. And certainly, if He did not operate internally on the human mind, there would be no propriety in asserting that 'He causeth the wisdom of the wise to perish, and the understanding of the prudent to be hid; that He poureth contempt upon princes, and causeth them to wander in the wilderness, where there is no way.' And to this He alludes, what we frequently read, that men are timorous, as their hearts are possessed with this fear. Thus, David departed from the camp of Saul, without the knowledge of any one; because a deep sleep from the Lord was fallen upon them all. But nothing can be desired more explicit than His frequent declarations, that He blinds the minds of men, strikes them with giddiness, inebriates them with the spirit of slumber, fills them with infatuation, and hardens their hearts. These passages, also, many refer to permission, as though, in abandoning the reprobate, God permitted them to be blinded by Satan. But that solution is too frivolous, as the Holy Spirit expressly declares that their blindness and infatuation are inflicted by the righteous judgment of God. He is said to have caused the obduracy of Pharaoh's heart, and also to have aggravated and confirmed it. Some elude the force of these expressions with a foolish cavil; that since Pharaoh himself is elsewhere said to have hardened his own heart, his own will is stated as the cause of his obduracy. As though these two things were at all incompatible with each other, that man should be actuated by God, and yet at the same time be active himself. But I retort on them their own objection; for if *hardening* denotes a bare permission, Pharaoh can not properly be charged with being the cause of his own obstinacy. Now, how weak and insipid would be such an interpretation, as though Pharaoh only permitted himself to be hardened. Besides the Scripture cuts off all occasion for such cavils. God says,—'I will harden his heart.' So also Moses says concerning the inhabitants of Canaan, that they marched forth to battle because the Lord had hardened their hearts; which is likewise repeated by another prophet,—' He turned their hearts to hate His people.' "* Here, then, the doctrine of the secret influencing of the heart of the reprobate, in order to carry out the reprobating decree by means of their obduracy, is clearly taught. The same doctrine is repeated by a much more modern author, as follows:—" Now, we maintain, that for God to settle everything, is the only right, as well as the only blessed, condition in which our world can be. But let us ask, what better would it make matters were God *not* to settle everything beforehand? This appears to us unspeakably worse."† In proof of this most universal settlement, or predestination, the author quotes, among other passages already considered, Rom. ix. 17,—" The scripture saith unto Pharaoh, even for this same purpose have I raised thee up, that I might show my power in thee, and that my name might be declared throughout all the

---

* Calvin's Institutes, book i. ch. xviii.
† Truth and Error, p. 46, 47.

earth." Such, then, are the ideas derived from those passages which it is our duty now to consider. Everything—even the hardening and destruction of those who become inveterately wicked, and are eternally lost—everything is "settled" from eternity, and, as settled in eternity, is carried out by the "secret influences" of God turning the heart to hatred, or to love, as suits His purpose! So He is to be viewed as *secretly* and intentionally hardening Pharaoh's heart, and the heart of his subjects, and as aggravating more and more this obduracy, at the same time that He was using the most apparently mighty *external* influence to change their hearts, so as to let His people go free from the fearful oppression under which they groaned. We have thus the doctrine clearly before us; and as by isolated texts it appears very strongly supported, we shall examine those texts as carefully as possible. But,—

I. LET US CONSIDER SOME OF THE VERY OBVIOUS OBJECTIONS THAT BEAR AGAINST THE DOCTRINE BEFORE US.

Here I might repeat those general objections that have been urged against the doctrine in other lectures, and in connection with other passages; but it will be more useful to take up those that are illustrated and confirmed by the history to which we require to refer. It is important, however, that the hearer should bear these general objections in mind.

1. *The doctrine which we have quoted, represents Jehovah as fighting with Himself.* Nothing can more clearly lie upon the very surface of the

statements, taken in connection with the history, than this most fatal idea. Mark, my hearer, the *first* thing that God is represented as doing, is turning the hearts of the Egyptians to hate His people, and to deal deceitfully with them (Ps. cv. 25). The immediate and necessary consequence of this is, that His people are oppressed. But what has given rise to this oppression? The doctrine before us answers, the Lord has given rise to it, in turning the hearts of the Egyptians against the Hebrews! But this serious oppression of the Hebrews, is said in the history to have ascended as a "*cry*" to the ears of Jehovah, and He comes forth for the purpose of delivering His people. Well, the *next* thing that God is represented by this doctrine as secretly doing, is the hardening of the heart of Pharaoh; and the necessary consequence of this is, that the king so hardened *will not* let the people be delivered in a direct manner. But the question arises again,—Why does Pharaoh refuse to let the people go? The doctrine replies,—Because God has hardened his heart! Here, then, Jehovah is the cause of this refusal. But the history tells us, that this refusal called for the display of mighty power on the part of God, that Pharaoh might be led at last to send the people away. Well, *externally*, Jehovah puts forth this mighty power, and performs wonders that make even the magicians of Egypt quail, and confess that it is God who strives with the king; but, *internally*, Jehovah still increases the obduracy of Pharaoh, so that he remains proof to all that is done! Is it not as clear as noon-day, that were this doctrine true, God would be *internally holding* and *externally driving*—that is, striving against Himself? It is surely one of the master-feats of delusion, that leads men to accept such monstrous doctrines, without even an attempt to understand the Scriptures of God in a more common-sense, not to say *God like* light. My hearer, is it possible that you can be blind to the deformity of a doctrine that ascribes to God the fearful folly of striving with Himself? Can you really regard Him as holding with the one hand and pushing with the other, and that in a matter where thousands of lives are sacrificed in the struggle? *Can* you believe, that *internally* He hardened the hearts of the Egyptians—turned them against His people—increased their desperate cruelty, and *externally* appeared to do the utmost to lead them to relent? Do not say that this is not the doctrine with which we have to do. Read again the words of the great Calvin himself, and you can not fail to see that it is the doctrine. And, moreover, it is impossible to *admit* the doctrine of predestination, and of secret hardening into the case, without seeing the full absurdity now pointed out. Is there not great need, then, for understanding the Scriptures more fully?

2. *The doctrine in question represents God as cruel in an infinite degree.* Let it not be forgotten that a whole *nation* of men are represented as held on the one hand, and on the other driven even to death, in this struggle of Jehovah with Himself. To turn the heart of any one to hate another, is an act of incomprehensible cruelty itself. To increase that hatred until it is ripened into deadly malice, is an act, for the description of which no words can

be found in the language of men. To *continue* to increase that obdurate malignity, after it has become so strong as to brave even death itself, or what was worse than death, the loss of the first-born, is, beyond conception, infamous: but all this is only a fraction of the cruelty *deliberately* ascribed to God by the doctrine with which we have now to do. This is only the *internal* part of it. You must add all the plagues of Egypt, and the drowning of their host in the Red Sea, and if you would take in the doctrine before us, you must ascribe the whole to God, and declare it the perfection of things, that thus He should settle everything! The difficulty is to comprehend how such a thought could be conceived, and, after it flashed upon the astounded mind, how it could be tolerated for a moment. And yet, my hearer, you must either take in this thought as God's truth, or what are we to make of the statement that "He turned their heart to hate His people?" What are you to make of the doctrine, that God foreordained whatsoever comes to pass? It will not do to say it is a "mystery." It is only a pity that this plea can not prevail, for it is but too little a mystery. It is a plain, palpable declaration, that God takes a nation between His hands, and pushing with the one hand, while drawing with the other, tears them to pieces! Surely, every hearer must be prepared to seek for truth of a very different complexion, in the words of the God of love.

3. *The doctrine which holds that God, by a secret inward influence, hardened the hearts of the Egyptians, represents God as deliberately deceiving*

them. It is most clear that *they* were not aware of the power of God hardening their hearts; and, it is further evident that the message with which Moses was *repeatedly* commissioned to address Pharaoh implied the contrary. Hear what he says, "Thus saith the Lord God of the Hebrews, Let my people go that they may serve me; for if thou refuse to let them go, and hold them still, behold the hand of the Lord is upon thy cattle which is in the field, upon the horses, upon the asses, upon the camels, upon the oxen, and upon the sheep; there shall be a grievous murrain." Exodus ix. 1-3. And again,—"As yet exaltest thou thyself against my people that thou wilt not let them go?" Exodus ix. 17. Can any man suppose that this would convey the idea to the mind of Pharaoh that all the while it was God who was secretly exalting him and hardening his already obdurate heart. There can not be the slightest doubt that the language would and *must* have produced the impression upon Pharaoh's mind, that his heart was hardened entirely *against* the *whole heart* of the God of the Hebrews. It must have led him to believe the *inmost desire* of that God to be, that he should yield; and there is not room for a doubt, that *if* Jehovah was *secretly hardening* Pharaoh's heart, He was also *openly* deceiving that king. Moreover, if Moses understood God as expositors have understood Him— Moses was sent to address Pharaoh in the distinct understanding that God was *secretly preventing* that on which He was *openly* and most mightily insisting. So, then, we must either believe that Moses understood nothing of the kind, or that he was sent to act the part of an infamous deceiver and hypocrite. It may be thought that I am using *strong language*—How can I do otherwise? How can you designate the most infamous hypocrisy but in calling it by its own name? Place *yourself*, my hearer, in Pharaoh's place. Suppose you had been dealt with as this doctrine represents him as treated, how would you have named the work of God and of Moses then? Your heart secretly hardened, and plague after plague inflicted because you would not yield! O! that the time were come when men would care for God even so much as they care for themselves. Even with this amount of piety they would cease from all indifference on such a subject as this—much more would they be disposed to search the Scriptures to see whether these things are so. Were this spirit only possessed in anything like a high degree, we can not conceive of much difficulty standing in the way of the most thorough and permanent clearing of these Scriptures from the least suspicion of containing the doctrines to which we have been now objecting.

II. LET US NOW ENDEAVOR TO ASCERTAIN THE REAL MEANING OF THE PASSAGES FROM WHICH THIS DOCTRINE IS DERIVED.

The course pursued by the man who is opposed to the divine authority of the Bible is, to insist that the passages do contain this doctrine, and so to throw from him both the Book and the ideas thus derived from it. The course pursued by others is to command, with proud and domineering indignation, the acceptance of the doctrine in its most horrid form, because *they say* it is that of God. The course I prefer is, to show by irresistible evidence, derived from the Bible itself, that it contains no such monstrosities—to reject the doctrine, and cling to the word of life and love. There are three classes of passages to be examined in pursuing this latter course.

1. *Consider those passages in which the* TRANSLATION ALONE *contains the semblance of the doctrine.* It is most important that, in every case, we should lay hold upon the real meaning of the writer, and also show where this doctrine of reprobation is founded without the shadow of ground.

Ps. cv. 25—"*He turned their hearts to hate His people,*" etc. There is no word for "HE" in the language of the Psalmist. It is the *creation* of the translator. The simple and most evident meaning of this verse is, "Their heart was turned to hate His people and to deal deceitfully with His servants." This is in perfect harmony with the context, and also with the history alluded to. Why should we have a dark and soul-blinding doctrine rested upon the creation of a translator? God blamed with turning the hearts of a whole nation to hatred, is no slight matter! It would need other ground than this.*

---

* As to Ps. cv. 25, there is not much difficulty. HAFAR is an intransitive verb as well as transitive, and, therefore, the verse may be translated,—"And their heart was turned," or "turned itself." See Lev. xiii. 3, 4, 13, 20, 55; Josh. vii. 8; Judges xx. 41; 2 Kings v. 26; where the verb has the nominative of "heart," as in Ps. cv. 25; Ps. lxxviii. 9; Judges xx. 39; 1

Exodus vii. 12—"*And He hardened Pharaoh's heart.*" Here the connection is such as, with the present translation, to ascribe the hardening of Pharaoh's heart to Aaron! He is the person named immediately before. But here again we have only the very awkward blunder of the translator on which to rest so serious a charge against Aaron. There is no word for "HE" in the original, and the simple meaning is that—"the heart of Pharaoh was hardened." To adduce the authority of the translators themselves, you have only to turn to the ninth chapter, and the thirty-fifth verse. Here the *very same words* that occur in the thirteenth are rendered, "And the heart of Pharaoh was hardened." Such, then, are two of the instances upon which we have seen considerable stress laid by the advocates of reprobation, and they are, most undeniably, the mere errors of the translator. Surely, it is ground of great suspicion in regard to expositors, when they found their creed, and insist upon it as absolutely divine, at the same time resting their

Sam. xxv. 12; 2 Chron. ix. 12. Hence *many* expositors render the verb intransitively in Ps. cv. 25. Dathe translates the expression,—"Hence being changed in mind." You will be delighted with Hammond's paraphrase of the verse,—"This great and signal goodness of God to the posterity of Jacob, in multiplying them so exceedingly, was a means to provoke the Egyptians' jealousy, and from fear they turned soon to hatred, and mischievous machinations against them, giving orders first for the oppressing them by burdens and hard labor (Ex. i. 11); and when they did not prevail to the lessening but increasing of them (v. 12), then enhancing the rigor of their servitude (v. 13, 14), and at length appointing all their male children to be killed as soon as they were born."—*Note by* PROFESSOR MORISON, *Kilmarnock*.

plea upon the translation of a phrase which is given differently in another place by the very translator on whom they depend. This leads us on to the second class of passages to which our attention requires to be turned.

2. *Let us consider those passages in which the real objects by which the heart is hardened are described.* By the careful consideration of these we will be prepared at once to see the meaning of the third class of texts in which the hardening of the heart appears to be directly ascribed to God Himself. By this consideration, also, we will be enabled to set aside the idea that the hearts of the Egyptians were hardened by "secret influences," exerted for that purpose. In Ex. i. 7–12, we have most clearly stated the motives that actuated the Egyptians in turning their hearts against the Hebrews, and the occurrences by which these motives were supplied. The words of the historian are these,—"And the children of Israel were fruitful, and increased abundantly, and multiplied, and waxed exceeding mighty; and the land was filled with them. Now there rose up a new king over Egypt which knew not Joseph. And he said unto his people, Behold, the people of the children of Israel are more and mightier than we. Come on, let us deal wisely with them; lest they multiply, and it come to pass, that, when there falleth out any war, they join also unto our enemies, and fight against us, and so get them up out of the land. Therefore they did set over them task-masters to afflict them with their burdens. And they built for Pharaoh treasure cities, Pithom and Raamses. But the more

they afflicted them, the more they multiplied and grew. And they were grieved because of the children of Israel." Here there is no possible room for "*secret influences.*" The Hebrews were made to prosper by Jehovah. *This prosperity* excited the envy of their foes and oppressors, and led them to deal deceitfully and murderously with the people of God. Jehovah gave the prosperity and increased it, and His doing so roused the worst feelings in the hearts of the vile oppressors under whose iron yoke the children of Jacob were already bound. He did not need to use any secret influence whatever to turn the hearts of the Egyptians to hate His people, and to deal subtly with His servants: He only gave His people prosperity, and *this* turned their hearts to a murderous hatred against them. It displays sad ignorance of human nature, and sad neglect of the passage before us, to hold that it was "*secret influences*" that hardened the heart of Pharaoh. It was *open* influence—it was the influence of prospering the Hebrews. This is distinctly and unhesitatingly stated by the inspired historian, and it is absurd to dispute it.

Mark, still further, the progress of events. Exodus ii. 23–25:—" And it came to pass, in process of time, that the king of Egypt died: and the children of Israel sighed by reason of the bondage, and they cried; and their cry came up unto God, by reason of the bondage. And God heard their groaning, and God remembered His covenant with Abraham, with Isaac, and with Jacob. And God looked upon the children of Israel; and God had respect unto them." The prosperity with which

Jehovah had blessed His people, through whom He had determined to bring about the salvation of men by the incarnation and death of Jesus, had roused the wicked envy and deadly hate of Egypt; and now these had risen to such a degree as to cry *loud* to Heaven for interference on behalf of the oppressed. Well, Jehovah did interfere. He prepared Moses, and sent him to be the deliverer of the Hebrews from the bondage of Egypt. Moses and Aaron, at last, by the command of their God, stood before Pharaoh, to make a very reasonable demand on behalf of the Israelites. What effect did this message of God produce? Read, and you will see that there was no need for *secret* hardening. Exodus v. 1-9:—"And afterward Moses and Aaron went in, and told Pharaoh, Thus saith the Lord God of Israel, Let my people go, that they may hold a feast unto me in the wilderness. And Pharaoh said, Who is the Lord, that I should obey His voice to let Israel go? I know not the Lord, neither will I let Israel go. And they said, The God of the Hebrews hath met with us; let us go, we pray thee, three days' journey into the desert, and sacrifice unto the Lord our God, lest He fall upon us with pestilence, or with the sword. And the king of Egypt said unto them, Wherefore do ye, Moses and Aaron, let the people from their works? Get you unto your burdens. And Pharaoh said, Behold the people of the land now are many, and ye make them rest them from their burdens. And Pharaoh commanded the same day the taskmasters of the people, and their officers, saying, Ye shall no more give the people straw to make brick, as heretofore: let them go and gather straw for themselves. And the tale of the bricks, which they did make heretofore, ye shall lay upon them; ye shall not diminish aught thereof: for they be idle; therefore, they cry, saying, Let us go and sacrifice to our God. Let there more work be laid upon the men, that they may labor therein; and let them not regard vain words." The demand for a small acknowledgment of freedom was more than sufficient "influence" to rouse the oppressor. It was like the note of "no slavery" upon the ear of an American slaveholder. It needed no secret or other influence whatever. The Hebrews themselves understood the principle which we are now evolving. Exodus v. 20, 21:—"And they met Moses and Aaron, who stood in the way, as they came forth from Pharaoh: And they said unto them, The Lord look upon you and judge; because ye have made our savor to be abhorred in the eyes of Pharaoh, and in the eyes of his servants, to put a sword in their hand to slay us." This was the true state of the case. This was the hardening of Pharaoh's heart. But Jehovah was not to yield though Pharaoh raged, and foamed, and murdered. No. There was one course open for infinite love and faithfulness, and this was to be pursued at all hazards, and in defiance of all consequences. The pursuing of this course was hardening Pharaoh's heart; but this was no reason why God should cease from it and cast off the cause of His people. No. The way of righteousness must not be left if the sinner is hardened in his sin by the pursuit of it. Man often does this, but God never will. He goes forward in that which is dictated by justice and love, whatever be the consequences to those who attempt to oppose. But the way in which Pharaoh's heart was hardened, and more especially the way in which that heart was increased in its obduracy, is clearly pointed out in Exodus vii. 10–12:—"And Moses and Aaron went in unto Pharaoh, and they did so as the Lord had commanded; and Aaron cast down his rod before Pharaoh, and before his servants, and it became a serpent. Then Pharaoh also called the wise men and the sorcerers; now the magicians of Egypt they also did in like manner with their enchantments. For they cast down every man his rod, and they became serpents; but Aaron's rod swallowed up their rods." And it follows as I have already corrected the translation (v. 13):— "And Pharaoh's heart was hardened." Was there any need of a secret influence here? The magicians supplied the place fully; and Pharoah called for them *in order that* they might fortify his mind against the plea of the oppressed. These lying magicians, by imitating the real miracle that had been performed, steeled the mind of the king against it. It is most fearful that any one should ascribe to the "secret influences" of God that which is so manifestly the fruit of the basest iniquity. The same thing is still clearer in the 22d verse of the same chapter. When the water of the river had been turned into blood, "the magicians did so with their enchantments; and Pharaoh's heart was hardened." Is it not most iniquitous to ascribe this result to God's "secret influences," when it is so manifestly the fruit of Pharaoh's wish, and of the lies of the magicians? Still more clear is the instance which we find in Exodus viii. 15: "But when Pharaoh saw that there was respite, he hardened his heart." God gave that "respite," and in doing so—not in the use of "secret influences"—he hardened the heart of Pharaoh. Mark, my hearer, that the respite is *expressly* stated as the motive by which Pharaoh's heart was hardened. In the 19th verse we are told that the magicians were compelled to desist from their lies, and to confess that "this was the finger of God," and *this*—no doubt as a galling disappointment—hardened the heart of the king. It is unnecessary that I should pursue this part of the subject further, under this head. It is most clear that, instead of requiring to have recourse to the miserable idea of God using secret influence to harden the heart of the king of Egypt, we have, in every instance, the *motive*, in view of which his mind became more obdurate, most distinctly stated. It is most important to bear this in mind, as it will clearly show us the principle on which to understand the statement that the Lord hardened Pharaoh's heart.

3. *Let us consider now those statements in which it is said that the Lord hardened the heart of Pharaoh.* We have already so far indicated the principle on which these must be understood, but it may be well just to take one or two illustrations. We shall take first, Stephen's preaching to the Jews. Before he began to declare the truth of God to his audience on the day of his martyrdom, that audience was composed of wicked men, but not of men prepared altogether to commit the act

of murder. His preaching roused their indignation. He, by that preaching, roused that indignation and malice. He hardened their hearts, and they murdered him as the consequence. Was Stephen wrong? Was he to blame for preaching the truth of God? The increase of wickedness was the direct result of his preaching—was he to blame? No man will say so. Did he use " secret influences" to rouse the malice of the crowd? Did God do so? No. There was no secret influence needed. It was only required to preach Jesus in their hearing; and Stephen, in doing so, made their malice rise to its murderous degree. Take another instance. A man of humanity goes into the Southern States of North America. He becomes acquainted with a minister there; and being a minister himself, he is invited to preach. He enters the pulpit, and after the usual exercises, during which the minds of his audience are calm, and deeply devotional to all appearance, and so far as they are conscious, he opens the Bible, and bids them turn for his text to Isa. lviii. 6, the last part of the verse: —" *that ye brake every yoke.*" He preaches from this a faithful anti-slavery sermon to slaveholders. What is the effect? Probably, ere he is halfway on with his sermon, he is dragged from the pulpit, and treated with infinitely greater hard-heartedness than that with which Moses was treated by Pharaoh. Now, who hardened their hearts against him?—who stirred them with murderous rage?— who turned their " devotional feelings" into madness and malignity? No one can doubt that it was himself. And was he to blame for this? Would it have been better that he should be dumb in the place where, above all others, he was required to speak out? No: silence in such a place is infamy; and yet by doing that which he was bound to do by every principle of truth and humanity, he hardened the hearts of his hearers. Just so was it with Jehovah in the case of Pharaoh. It was ANTI-SLAVERY EFFORTS that hardened Pharaoh's heart, and these alone. But it may be well to take up the passages particularly.

Exodus iv. 21.—"And the Lord said unto Moses, When thou goest to return into Egypt, see that thou do all those wonders before Pharaoh which I have put in thine hand; but I will harden his heart, that he shall not let the people go." Here most distinctly the intimation of God is in perfect accordance with the principle we have explained. This intimation was intended to prevent the consequences of disappointment in Moses. The command given to him was in substance this: "Desist not from the course pointed out, though you will see that it is hardening the heart of Pharaoh, and *increasing* his determination not to part with the enslaved." This was a most important and most *necessary* warning to Moses. Had it not been for this warning, like many another poor advocate of the oppressed, he would have been silent with confusion when he saw that he was rousing the malignity instead of gaining the heart of the king. O! how many have needed this *very* imitation! They have turned out useless in every good work, because they neglected to count on the worst. When they saw that God by their means was hardening hearts, they gave up

God's way, and took to their own. Moses was warned against this. He was commanded to be sure to carry out his commission, though he would see that this was its effect. This truth is confirmed by the declaration of God in chap. iii. 19. There He says to Moses: "I am sure the king of Egypt will not let you go, but* by a mighty hand." He takes the greatest care to fortify the mind of his emancipator against the disappointment which He knew he would at first encounter. His great object was to insure his perseverance in the cause of freedom, in the face of all possible obstacles.

Exodus vii. 3, 4.—"And I will harden Pharaoh's heart, and multiply my signs and my wonders in the land of Egypt. But Pharaoh shall not hearken unto you, that I may lay my hand upon Egypt, and bring forth mine armies, and my people the children of Israel out of the land of Egypt, by great judgments." This passage is already explained by the application of the same principle that is applied above, only there is one base mistranslation without the shadow of a warrant in the original. Jehovah says literally, "*and* I will lay my hand upon Egypt," not "*that I may* lay my hand upon Egypt." His whole words to Moses are these, verse 2,—"Thou shalt speak all that I command thee, and Aaron, thy brother, shall speak unto Pharaoh, that he send the children of Israel out of his land; but" (and here is introduced again the warning to prevent disappointment in Moses), "I will harden Pharaoh's heart, and multiply my signs and wonders in the land of Egypt; and Pharaoh will not hearken unto

* This is the marginal reading.

you; and I will lay my hand upon Egypt." There is no idea here that Pharaoh's deafness was intended by God to give Him an opportunity of laying His hand upon Egypt. There was simply and strongly laid before Moses, that which was necessary in the circumstances, to lead him to proceed with the work of emancipation. One of the most invaluable of moral principles is evolved by this history—that of counting the cost of a great moral movement, and of going on with it steadily, even if hell should appear to be brought upon earth by the progress of truth.

Exodus ix. 11, 12.—"And the magicians could not stand before Moses because of the boil: for the boil was upon the magicians, and upon all the Egyptians. And the Lord hardened the heart of Pharaoh, and he hearkened not unto them; as the Lord had spoken unto Moses." Here the meaning is manifest from the connection. The magicians were discomfited, and compelled to flee from the face of Moses; and even this hardened Pharaoh's heart. The facts that ought to have laid him in the dust only enraged him more.

Exodus x. i.—"And the Lord said unto Moses, Go in unto Pharaoh: for I have hardened his heart, and the heart of his servants, that I might show these my signs before him." This verse is partly explained on the same principles with that of the others. Jehovah had only hardened the heart of Pharaoh, by doing that which it was right and most necessary for Him to do—and by doing that which was fitted in itself to produce the very opposite result. This verse is made much more clear, however, by reading it, according to the connection, with a parenthesis. "Go in unto Pharaoh (for I have hardened his heart), that I may show these signs before him, and that thou mayest tell in the ears of thy son, and of thy son's son, what things I have wrought in Egypt." This is in most strict accordance with the letter, as well as with the spirit of the original, and shows, not that God had made Pharaoh wicked that He might show wonders, but that Moses was to go in unto Pharaoh, that the wonders might appear, and that he was to go in *because* all that had been yet done, had only hardened the heart of the king. It is impossible to bring a valid objection against this interpretation; and you can not take the one opposed to it, without representing God and Moses as leagued to effect the most fearful deception; for, read the 3d and 4th verses,—" And Moses and Aaron came in unto Pharaoh, and said unto him, Thus saith the Lord God of the Hebrews, How long wilt thou refuse to humble thyself before me? let my people go, that they may serve me: Else, if thou refuse to let my people go, behold, to-morrow will I bring the locusts into thy coast." I can not, in the face of these, take a different view of the passage from that given; and I must believe that every hearer, who looks out at all to the connection of the passage, will feel himself *shut up* to the same. Thus, we still see, even in these passages, the glorious truth, that "God is love." Aye, we shall yet see "love" even to Pharaoh. The 20th verse of this chapter is explained on the same principle, "and the Lord hardened Pharaoh's heart." After all that he did, *this* was the only result. The same principle applies also to the 11th chapter and 10th verse, also to the words occurring in xiv. 4, also 8th and 17th. By the slightest care, it will be seen, to the very last, that the hardening of the hearts of the Egyptians, was the effect of that which it was absolutely necessary for God to do, in order to deliver His oppressed people. The truth of these remarks may be confirmed, by particular attention, to the hardening of the Egyptians, by which they were led into the sea and drowned. Exodus xiv. 16, 17,—" But lift up thy rod, and stretch out thine hand over the sea, and divide it; and the children of Israel shall go on dry ground through the midst of the sea. And I, behold, I will harden the hearts of the Egyptians, and they shall follw them: and I will get me honor upon Pharaoh, and upon all his host, upon his chariots, and upon his horsemen." Here, it is perfectly clear, that the opening of the sea determined the Egyptians to pursue their former slaves into the midst of it, and this desperate wickedness *called aloud* for that judgment by which the waves of the ocean completed their ruin. It is impossible thus to trace the history of these events, and to see their effects, according to laws which we see in operation every day around us, and not to abhor the error by which Jehovah is made to appear as *secretly and intentionally* preventing the repentance of the Egyptians. It would be every whit as just, to ascribe the living and murderous rage with which an American slaveholder pursues his slave, to the secret instigation of God. It is the escape of the slave, and it may be some striking interposition of God in his behalf, that *maddens the malignity* of his oppressor. The theory of *secret influence* in such a case, is worthy of the darkest ages; and yet the same theory, in the case of Pharaoh, is no better.

I have thus at large, and particularly, reviewed the case of the Egyptians, as recorded in Exodus, and it remains to consider the words of Paul very briefly, as I have done this at large elsewhere.* Romans ix. 17, 18,—"For the scripture saith unto Pharaoh, Even for this same purpose have I raised thee up, that I might show my power in thee, and that my name might be declared throughout all the earth. Therefore hath He mercy on whom He will have mercy, and whom He will He hardeneth." The explanation which we have already had, shows how God is neither unrighteous nor unkind, when He hardens whom He will. It was the object of Paul to show this, in vindication of God, as hardening the hearts of the Jews by the mission and proclamation of Jesus. He shows that He was hardening them, just as He had hardened the Egyptians, by carrying out before them the great deliverance; and though he proceeded with this till their obstinacy had become desperate, he was perfectly righteous. He could not turn from a

---

* I have omitted the consideration of several texts that would otherwise have fallen under notice in this discussion, because they are fully treated in my other little volume, entitled, "Light out of Darkness." The reader will permit me to refer to that for a full consideration of this passage of the Epistle to the Romans.

right course to please or soothe them. He could not but proclaim a crucified Saviour, though this should rouse them to the most fearful and self-destroying frenzy. It was *thus alone* that He willed to harden.

But this passage is made much more clear, when we remember that the "*raising up*" of Pharaoh was his *recovery from a deadly illness*. It was after the plague of the boils that Jehovah addressed him as quoted by Paul, and thus, instead of God saying that He had created, or exalted Pharaoh to the throne to show His power in destroying him, He was telling him that He had raised him from the bed of death, in order that still further He might show him His power and goodness for his repentance. By reading the account in Exodus, this most clearly appears. Having thus lengthened out this lecture, I must close with only a few remarks. Let it not be forgotten that the most gracious dealings of God have two opposite effects upon men—they harden as well as melt the soul. Nor let it be forgotten that Jehovah will not turn from a right course, because He knows that He is hardening the impenitent sinner; and O! my hearer, especially beware lest you occupy the position of him whom Jehovah's dealings harden. Depend on this—the theory of a "*secret* influence" will not stand in the great day of the Lord. You will see then that all on God's part was open, and full of love, and, if all has only hardened you, it will be a fearful thing to remember what has been done for you, and see the effect produced. Open your mind to the melting power of the love of God—"The Holy

Spirit saith, Oh! that to-day you would hear His voice—harden not your hearts." He is talking of the things of Christ, and showing them to you now. Do, I beseech you, turn your mind to the great atonement—study it as a guilty soul may be expected to study the acknowledgment of its ransom paid. You will—you must be blessed in such a study.

LECTURE XII.

PREDESTINATION AND THE DEATH OF THE REPROBATE.

THE passages to which I request attention in this lecture are two. In the first, we have an account of the death of the sons of Eli; and in that account the following words occur,—1 Sam. ii. 25: "If one man sin against another, the judge will judge him; but if a man sin against the Lord, who shall entreat for him." These are the solemn words of warning which Eli addressed to his wicked sons; and it is added,—"Notwithstanding they hearkened not to the voice of their father, because the Lord would slay them." The second passage to which I call attention is that in which we have an account of the death of Ahab, king of Israel. In the account of that occurrence, we have the following words: 1 Kings xxii. 20-22—"And the Lord said, Who shall persuade Ahab, that he may go up and fall at Ramoth-gilead? And one said on this manner, and another said on that manner. And there came forth a spirit, and stood before the Lord, and said, I will persuade him. And the Lord said unto him, Wherewith? And he said, I will go forth, and I will be a lying spirit in the mouth of all his prophets. And He said, Thou shalt persuade him, and prevail also; go forth and do so." The doctrine which is founded upon these and kindred passages, so far as foundation is sought for it in the Bible, is, that God predetermines the miserable death of certain men, and that not in the way of permitting it, but in the way of securing it, and *preventing their repentance*, in order that this ruin which He has predestined for them may not be averted. The doctrine, however, will be best stated in the words of its own great advocate. These are as follows,—" It often occurs in the sacred history, that whatever comes to pass proceeds from the Lord, as the defection of the ten tribes, the death of the sons of Eli, and many events of a similar kind." Again, " God intends the deception of that perfidious king Ahab; the devil offers his service for that purpose; he is sent, by a positive commission, to be a lying spirit in the mouth of all the prophets. If the blinding and infatuation of Ahab be a divine judgment, the pretense of bare permission disappears, for it would be ridiculous for a judge merely to permit, without decreeing what should be done, and commanding his officers to do it." These portions of sacred history now before us are given in defense of the following strong statement:—" The modesty of those who are alarmed at the appearance of absurdity, might, perhaps, be excusable, if they did not attempt to vindicate the divine justice from all accusation by a pretense utterly destitute of any foundation in truth! They consider it absurd that a man should be blinded by the will and command of God, and afterwards be punished for his blindness. They, therefore, evade the difficulty, by alleging that it happens only by permission, and not by the will of God; but God Himself, by the most unequivocal declarations, rejects this subterfuge. That man, however, can effect nothing but by the secret will of God, and even deliberate on nothing, but what He hath previously decreed and determines by His secret direction, is proved by express and innumerable testimonies."* The passages before us are part of these express and innumerable testimonies;" and as it is most unnecessary to quote farther, we must proceed directly to the removal of that fearful load which the doctrine of universal predestination has thus cast upon the word and character of our God. Surely, no one who reflects on the importance of His glory can deem our work unnecessary.

I. LET US CONSIDER SOME OF THE OBJECTIONS THAT BEAR VERY MANIFESTLY AGAINST THE DOCTRINE NOW BEFORE US.

It is right and proper to state objections when we feel their force upon our own minds; but it is our bounden duty to do so, when we proceed to alter and reject the opinions of others; and it may not be out of place to observe likewise that those objections which we are about to state are such that, in view of them, every man is *bound to seek* at least some interpretation of the passages in hand different from that which is given in the doctrines just quoted.

1. *The doctrine before us represents God as preferring the death of these three men to their repent-*

---

* Calvin's Institutes, book i. ch. xviii.

ance. This lies upon the very surface of the doctrine. He is made to appear in want of some one to accomplish the destruction of Ahab, and as withholding light, and blinding the minds of the sons of Eli, because His secret desire was that neither of these parties should repent, but that they should die. Now, it is unnecessary again to remind my hearer that this is contrary to the very oath of God Himself. It is the *very reverse* of the declaration that He makes on oath, " As I live, saith the Lord God, I have no pleasure in the death of the wicked; BUT RATHER that the wicked turn from his way and live." This declaration is *fatal* to the doctrine before us. Jehovah's preference is seen here to be for the LIFE, and not for the DEATH of the wicked. " The Lord is not slack concerning His promise, as some men count slackness, but is long-suffering to usward, not willing that any should perish, but that all should come to repentance." What, then, is God's preference ? Is it the death of the wicked ? So says the doctrine before us; and, in doing so, it runs against the omnipotent declaration of God Himself. I hold, then, that on the ground of this most manifest objection, every man is bound by all the obligations that God has laid upon him *to seek for* a different solution of the passage in question. It is not a favorite creed that demands this of each of us ; but it is demanded by the sacredness of the character and truth of Jehovah Himself.

2. *The doctrine before us represents God as purposely aggravating the doom of the wicked.* We can not, if we accept this doctrine, stop short by believing that God prefers the death of the wicked

to their repentance; we are forced on to the idea that He prefers that their death should be of the most horrid kind. He could have slain the sons of Eli *before* they rejected the solemn counsel of their father, as well as after it. But it is held that the cup of their iniquity was not then full. Their punishment would have been less then, but, as appears from this doctrine, God desired that it should be greater. So with Ahab. He was predestinated to death; he had far less sin before he went to Ramoth-gilead than after; and if it had been simply his death that was desired, He might have been slain then; but, as appears from the doctrine before us, it was an aggravated death that God desired for Ahab! Alas! men may cry out "mystery" when such an opinion is assailed. It is a wretched defense. We must drag the vile and hideous monster error forth from his den of mystery, and let him live, if he can, under the rays of the Sun of Righteousness. It is impossible. Subjected to the light of the glory of God, as it shines in the face of Christ Jesus, and glistens in the tears with which that face was bedewed, because of the death of the wicked in Jerusalem, that error must die. It is in mystery alone and in darkness the doctrine can live. You are bound, my hearer, to find another interpretation of the word of God, or if you can not find that, at least to refrain from giving such an one as that before us.

3. *The doctrine in question represents God as a deceiver.* These are the express words already quoted; "God intends the deception of that perfidious king Ahab." Now, is my hearer prepared to be-

lieve that God can intend the deception of any one? Is he prepared to receive an interpretation of the Scriptures which actually represents the God of truth as giving a commission to deceive? My hearer, I know not, as I speak, what may be your state of mind in hearing; but of this I am sure, that you can not read such language without feeling that *there must be something wrong* in connection with it. If we are really to believe that God may deceive, then we may follow His example; for that which is right in itself for Him, can not be wrong in itself for us; and thus, to follow the example of God, would be to become deceivers. O! it is sickening to see the extent to which a misleading theory will carry off the mind of man—to hear one of the friends of the true God actually declaring that He intended to deceive! We shall see that the passage of sacred history from which this notion is derived, not only gives it no countenance, but carries its contradiction upon the very face of it. In the meantime, it is most important to feel the full force of the objections applied to the doctrine itself. The Spirit says, "God can not be tempted with evil, *neither tempteth He any man.*" How does this agree with the doctrine before us? How does the alleged deception of Ahab agree with this declaration of God Himself? Can you, my hearer, reconcile them? Can you regard them both as true? Depend upon it, you can not *thus* meet the difficulties of the unbeliever, *nor will you be able thus to meet the infidel suggestions that may yet assail your own mind, it may be in a dying hour.* O! it is incalculably important that you should see intelligently the truth and consistency of the Book of God.

4. *The doctrine in question is contradicted upon the very face of one of the passages under consideration.* Only read and reflect upon the whole account of Ahab's death, and then ask yourself the question, Could God intend to deceive him?' Mark the words of Micaiah, the only true man of God present among the prophets that prophesied to Ahab, 1 Kings xxii. 14—" And Micaiah said, As the Lord liveth, what the Lord saith unto me, that will I speak." Here, then, was a man, and he the only one who had the word of God to communicate, and hear what the Lord directs him to say. Is it such as could deceive Ahab? Is it such as can indicate an intention on the part of God to deceive him so as to induce him to go up to Ramoth-gilead? Only ask yourself if you would have been induced to go up and fall in Ramoth-gilead by such a statement as that made to Ahab? On what ground here can we rest the idea that "God intended to deceive that perfidious king Ahab?" Manifestly upon no ground but that which is found in a most *partial* and *false* quotation from the passage. It is most clear, as we shall see, that the whole testimony of the prophet of God went to undeceive Ahab, and also, that the king *felt* undeceived by that testimony; yet Micaiah's was the only testimony that came from the Lord. We shall find occasion, however, to pursue this subject further afterward. What I insist on now is, that these four objections which I have stated are *more* than sufficient to convince any man that, if he has taken the view of those passages

which is given in the doctrine we have quoted, he has not understood them aright. If these objections are reflected on, they will inevitably show, that, whatever be the meaning of these scriptures, it can not be that which is thus put upon them. This prepares us for the examination of those portions of the Bible that we may understand them according to the manifest intention of the Spirit of God.

II. LET US EXAMINE THE PASSAGES BEFORE US THAT WE MAY SEE THEIR TRUE MEANING.

As in all other parts of the Bible, when studied aright, we shall find in these the opening heart and outflowing goodness and mercy of our God.

1. *Let us turn our attention to* 1 *Samuel* ii. 25. In our "authorized version" the meaning of this text is, that the sons of Eli did not hearken to the counsel of their father, "*because* the Lord would slay them." This rendering makes it appear that the wish of God to slay them, was the *cause* of their not listening to their father; and it implies that had the Lord wished them to live, they would have hearkened and obeyed. It will appear at once, however, that the whole of this idea rests upon the word "BECAUSE." Let that be altered and this prop of the horrid doctrine already quoted is removed. Now, we may hold, with the most perfect safety, the truth, that unless that word "*because*" be the *necessary*, and *inevitable* translation of the original, as used by the historian, we ought, under the force of the objections already stated, to

understand and translate it otherwise. We can scarcely be wrong in supposing that every right mind, on reading the passage as it now stands, will be led to ask,—" Is it impossible for that particle to be translated otherwise?" We shall see immediately that it is neither impossible nor very difficult to prove that it may be rendered differently. (1.) *Mark the force of Eli's words.* They are literally as follows:—" If a man sin against a man, God will condemn him; and if a man sin against Jehovah, *who shall entreat for him?*" This was the strongest mode in which he could state the certainty of the doom of those who persisted in sinning as his sons had done—directly against the Lord. By the unanswerable question he affirms, in the strongest manner, that the Lord would put them to death. The sons of Eli stood in the place of mediators between the people and God; and thus had more *directly* to do with Him than the rest of their countrymen, and the declaration of their father was that if God was pleased to devote to death those who simply sinned against their fellow-men, and stood at a greater distance as it were from God, how much more would He please to devote them to the same doom. His " voice," then, was "that the Lord would slay them." This was the solemn warning of Eli to his sons, and it was *this* they would not hear. The passage properly translated runs thus: " Yet they would not hear the voice of their father —THAT the Lord would slay them." That is, they would not listen to the fact that Jehovah would certainly put them to death. The temptation of Satan was in their hearts as a loved principle—" Ye shall not surely die." It will be seen that this rendering of the historian's words completely removes all difficulty from the passage, and it remains only for me to prove that the translation is unquestionably true. (2.) Mark, then, that the particle (כי) rendered "*because*" in the authorized version has very commonly the meaning of "THAT" in the connection I have noted. In order to make this matter of no doubt to the mind of the hearer, I shall notice a few of the instances, in multitudes of which it occurs in this sense. Gen. xiv. 14—"And when Abraham heard THAT (כי) his brother was taken." Gen. xxx. 33—"*Because* (כי) the Lord hath heard THAT (כי) I was hated." Here the particle occurs in both uses, and can not be rendered in only one. Gen. xxxix. 15—"And it came to pass when he heard THAT (כי) I lifted up my voice." Gen. xlii. 2—"And he said, Behold I have heard THAT (כי) there is corn in Egypt." Gen. xliii. 25—"*For* (כי) they heard THAT (כי) they should eat bread there." Here, again, the particle occurs in both uses. Numb. xiv. 14—"For they have heard THAT (כי) thou, Lord, art among this people—*that* (כי understood) thou art seen face to face—and that (כי understood again) thy cloud standeth over them—and *that* thou goest before them," etc. It is unnecessary to multiply instances, as this must be admitted by all who know anything of the uses of the word at all, to be an undoubted, and most common use of it. The particle thus used, simply points out *that* which has been seen, or known, or heard, or remembered, according to the remark of Gesenius, which I give in the note below.* The plain meaning of the passage, then, is, that the sons of Eli would not hear that the Lord was prepared to put them to death. Unlike the Ninevites who turned from their wickedness when such a declaration was made to them, these base men discredited altogether the warning voice. Thus is the dreary error of God keeping their eyes shut, that He might kill them, thrown off like an unhallowed load from this portion of the word of God.†

Surely, my hearer, it is a relief to your mind, if

---

* GESENIUS says of this particle (כי) " So after verbs of seeing, Gen. i. 4, 10, 12 ; iii. 6 : of hearing, Gen. xiv. 14 ; xxix. 33 ; xxxix. 15 : of knowing, Gen. xxii. 12 ; xxiv. 14 ; xlii. 33 : of pointing out, Gen. iii. 11 ; xii. 18 ; Psalms l. 6 ; xcii. 10 : of demanding, Isa. i. 12 : of forgetting, Job xxxix. 15." He gives these instances as kindred with Gen. i. 10, " *And God saw* this, viz., *that it was good.*" The Greek word corresponding to כי ($\delta\tau\iota$) has the same signification. See Robinson's Lex. largely on the word.

† Our "authorized version" is seen to be the more at fault in this glaring case, from the fact that there are, *three* other uses of the particle (כי), that may be well justified. Tarnovius and Noldius render it "*although,*" and give the sense thus :—" Notwithstanding they would not hearken unto the voice of their father, *although* the Lord should slay them. Geier, Pfeiffer, Glassius and Horne translated it "therefore," and give the sense—" Notwithstanding they hearkened not to the voice of their father, *therefore* the Lord would slay them." *Both* of these uses of the particle are actually acknowledged by our translators themselves, and thus, though they were not supported by instances as they are, they might still be pleaded against the translation in the common version. I prefer the one I have given because of its being by far the best established use of the particle, and one regarding which there is no room left to doubt. The identical rendering I have given is also given by D. Schmid.

it also has been loaded with this horrid error, to discover, at least in another instance, that the God of the Bible has been falsely accused, and that this dark and soul-distressing doctrine has no shadow of support beyond the narrow and misguiding prejudice of an erring translator. O! see your God as a God of justice indeed, but also, and in that very justice, a God of changeless, endless love. Yes it was love even to Eli's sons to warn them—to make a last effort to redeem their souls.

2. *Let us now direct our attention to* 1 *Kings*, xxii. There are several points of the narrative here given which it is important to keep specially in view.

(1.) Ahab was a king of habitual wickedness. So much was this the case, that Micaiah, the prophet of God, never spoke good of him. His whole proceedings were characterized by wickedness. The very opening of this chapter shows that even three years of peace was too much for him, and he must have war.

(2.) This king had about four hundred prophets, on whose *favorable word* he could depend. What must have been the character of these prophets? They could prophecy to please a wicked king. That they were *habitually* animated by the spirit of falsehood there can be no doubt. They are called Ahab's prophets—not prophets of God. Such were the men called together by Ahab when he wished to go to war upon Ramoth-gilead.

(3.) It is manifest that Jehoshaphat had no confidence in these prophets of Ahab. He did not say so directly, as this would have given grievous offense; but he said, "Is there not A PROPHET OF JE-HOVAH besides, that we might inquire of him?" It is most clear that the king of Judah regarded the parasitical prophets of Ahab as no authority in a case of need. He could not be deceived by them. Nor did Ahab much value their testimony; for instead of resenting the very plain condemnation of his prophets implied in the question of Jehoshaphat, he answered that there was a prophet of the Lord of whom they might inquire. Now, if God had intended to deceive Ahab, as Calvin says, would He have woven so thin a web of deception as this? Even thus far the truth is evident, that God had provided a light sufficient to *undeceive* Ahab in the person of His own prophet. How can any man, with the facts of the case before him, think that it was God's intention to deceive Ahab so as to accomplish his ruin?

(4.) The messenger sent for Micaiah shows that the whole matter of the prophecy of the four hundred was a hypocritical farce, and known to be such. How otherwise could he have exhorted the prophet of God to speak as the others had done? Micaiah gave an answer that placed him at once infinitely above the suspicion of hypocrisy, and made his word, as it had been in time past, the only word of weight that the king of Israel was to hear. Ahab knew that this was the *only man* then prepared to let him know the truth, and he did at the hazard of his life speak that truth.

(5.) Mark the *manner* in which Micaiah spake when brought before the king. His first words are, "Go and prosper, for the Lord shall deliver it into the hand of the king." How did he utter these words? Did he speak so as to deceive the king, or so as to undeceive him? The question is answered at once in the reply of Ahab. "And the king said unto him, How many times shall I adjure thee that thou tell me nothing but that which is true in the name of the Lord?" Why should Ahab speak thus? If Micaiah had not by his *manner* clearly indicated that he was speaking ironically, could Ahab have felt any ground for this question? Had the God of this prophet *intended to deceive* Ahab, would he not have led him to speak so solemnly as to put away all ground for such a question?

(6.) Mark the reply of Micaiah when commanded to speak the truth, and after he had assumed a solemn aspect: "I saw all Israel scattered upon the hills as sheep that have no shepherd. And the Lord said, These have no master: let them return every man to his house in peace." Now, my hearer, how does the statement look that "God intended to *deceive* that perfidious king, Ahab?" Does it appear a truth or a falsehood? I demand, if you have given ear to that doctrine, that you answer the question to Him, to the slander of whose holy name you have listened. How *could* it ever enter the mind of man, reading the actual history, that there was on the part of God an intention to deceive that king? *Was the king deceived?* No; he rushed *in the face of* the warning of God to meet his ruin. He went to death, and he went to meet it with his eyes open as the plain statement of the truth could make them. It is impossible to designate the conduct of those who make it appear from this passage that God intended to deceive Ahab, and commissioned Satan for that purpose. It is the founding of one of the most hideous of errors where not only it has no place to stand, but where it has its flat contradiction upon the very face of the narrative.

(7.) Mark the skill of the *parable* by which Micaiah seeks to undeceive the mind of Ahab. The learned Horne, in his Introduction to the Critical Study of the Scriptures, has the following remark: "The address of Micaiah to the two confederated kings in verses 19–23 is not a real representation of anything done in the heavenly world, as if the Almighty were at a loss for expedients, or had any hand in the sins of His creatures; but it is a mere parable, and only tells, in figurative language, what was in the womb of providence, the events that were shortly to take place, and the *permission*, on the part of God, for these agents to act. Micaiah did not choose to tell the angry and imperious Ahab, that all his prophets were liars; but he represents the whole by this parable, and says the same truths in language equally forcible, but less offensive." *
The parable is as follows (verses 19–23) :—" And he said, Hear thou, therefore, the word of the Lord. I saw the Lord sitting on His throne, and all the host of heaven standing by Him on His right hand and on His left. And the Lord said, Who shall persuade Ahab, that he may go up and fall at Ramoth-gilead? And one said on this manner, and another said on that manner. And there came forth a spirit, and stood before the Lord, and said, I will

* Horne's Intro. part ii. b. ii. ch. xiii. § v. 16.

persuade him. And the Lord said unto him, Wherewith? And he said, I will go forth, and I will be a lying spirit in the mouth of all his prophets. And He said, Thou shalt persuade him, and prevail also; go forth, and do so. Now, therefore, behold, the Lord hath put a lying spirit in the mouth of all these thy prophets, and the Lord hath spoken evil concerning thee." Can any one read that parable, and remember it was stated to Ahab by the prophet of God, and then take in the idea that the Lord intended to deceive that king? Such an idea is out of the question, and no man could ever have gathered it from this passage, unless He had first of all determined, by one way or another, to have it taught in the Bible. O! let us rejoice that a faithful and true God is faithful and true, and deeply compassionate, even to Ahab, the impious king; and that, instead of intending to deceive him, He did the very utmost that could be done, and that at the risk of the life of His faithful servant, to show him his danger, and to lead him to repentance. Yes, my hearer, though you are baser even than Ahab, God will neither deceive you, nor leave you to Satan, nor feel cold and indifferent to you, but will continue to strive to the last, even until He will truly say, "What could have been done more for you that I have not done?" (Is. v. 4.) It is most clear that, to the very last, He warned Ahab, and that had not the king persisted in the face of the very clearest light, he would have turned to his God and been "abundantly pardoned." Instead of this, he ordered the servant of God, who told him the truth, to be imprisoned, and went forth evidently under the conviction of guilt, for he disguised himself in the meanest manner, and showed all the symptoms of a conscience-stricken soul.

III. LET US LEARN A FEW PRACTICAL AND IMPORTANT LESSONS FROM THIS SUBJECT.

It is too important that we should lay it aside by merely understanding its meaning. Let us see our God, as He appears shining forth from the darkness in which His character has been shrouded by the doctrines with which we have had to do in this lecture.

1. *We learn the amazing forbearance of Jehovah, even unto the basest of sinners.* We have an account of the guilt of Eli's sons, from which the soul turns away with loathing; and yet, God did not yield to deliver them to death, until they had resisted His Spirit, in the last solemn warning that could be tendered them. He bore with them to the last. It was only after *mercy itself* called for their removal from the earth, that they might not continue as a pestilence among the people, that the Lord yielded them to the sword of the enemy. The same is most clear in the case of Ahab. He is said to have "sold himself to commit iniquity;" and yet, the Lord did not leave him. Instead of leaving him, He continued to warn him to the very last, and even then Ahab went to his death in the face of the clearest light. O! my hearer, can you read these narratives, and see the wondrous forbearance of your God, and not pant for the promotion of the knowledge of His love? Above all, can

you doubt the fullness and freeness of His mercy *to you*, when you see its vast extent to those most wicked of men? How much must His delight be to receive the returning sinner, when He strives so long and so powerfully with those who are determined never to return.

2. *We learn from this subject the fearful influence of the doctrine of universal predestination.* Only try to conceive of the immense forbearance and love of God to these wicked men being converted into an eternal determination to destroy them! Can you grasp the fearful magnitude of that transformation? Yet such is the transformation effected by the doctrine in question. From the very highest and most glorious eminence of heavenly light, shining in that compassion that feels for even Ahab, the name of God is cast down into that impenetrable darkness in which He is supposed to employ Satan, to deceive still further the doomed monarch, in order to make his end more fearful than it would otherwise have been! Surely, that doctrine that leads to the conversion of the light of eternal love into the gloom of eternal hatred, must yet become detested by every soul in which the last spark of reverence for God has not been utterly extinguished.

3. *We learn from this subject how deeply needful it is for us to search the Bible for ourselves.* Many have cast off Christianity because they have allowed others to search the Bible for them. They have been, by this means, cheated out of an eternal inheritance. They have rightly concluded that God can not join hands with Satan in deceiving any one;

but they have taken the idea at second hand, that the Bible teaches such a fearful thought; and hence, they have cast off the Bible. Without even a star in the black night of their infidelity, they have launched their eternal spirits upon a dread uncertainty, to sink in everlasting darkness; and all this simply for want of searching the Scriptures *for themselves.* O! my dear hearer, let me assure you, from experience, that the searching of the Bible is a work of rich reward. The more carefully, honestly, and prayerfully you do so, the more will your spirit be enriched with the fullness of God; whereas, if you carelessly take the Bible at second hand, you may speedily find your souls dashed among the rocks of a miserable skepticism. And do not forget that it will be the most humbling position a soul can possibly occupy, to stand at the judgment-seat, endeavoring to hide behind some far-famed expositor, who has been instrumental in leading you to think falsely of the Book of God. Stand on the Rock of Ages, and that on your own feet; and while you feel the firmness and safety of your position, you will be constrained to invite others to stand there also, that they may be blessed as well as you.

LECTURE XIII.

PREDESTINATION AND A FOREORDAINED JUDGMENT.

The passage of scripture to which your attention is required, under this head, is that found in the Epistle of Jude, at the fourth verse : "For there are certain men, crept in unawares who were before of old ordained to this condemnation." These words have for many generations, and by thousands of men, been regarded as teaching the doctrine of reprobation from eternity. As proof of this fact, we have only to turn to the acknowledged standard which constitutes the *Confession* of the vast majority of professing Christians in this land of Bibles. The verse before us is quoted as a proof of the statement, that " the rest of mankind " (that is, besides the eternally chosen), " God was pleased, according to the unsearchable counsel of His own will, whereby He extendeth or withholdeth mercy as He pleaseth, for the glory of His sovereign power over His creatures, to pass by, and to ordain them to dishonor and wrath for their sin, to the praise of His glorious justice." Such, then, is the doctrine that is believed to be taught by Jude in the text before us. According to it, millions yet unborn are ordained to eternal death! It is surely the duty of every man to sift such a doctrine, and especially to see most carefully to it, that the word of God does teach the idea, if it is to be held at all. He incurs no slight responsibility who holds such a view, if God has never taught him to do so.

I. LET US CONSIDER SOME SCRIPTURAL OBJECTIONS TO SUCH AN INTERPRETATION OF THE PASSAGE.

The doctrine is, that the final condemnation of those who perish eternally, has been a matter of eternal foreordination, so that they may be said to have been condemned from eternity to eternity. It is the natural and necessary inference from the doctrine, that whatever Jehovah foreknows will take place, He has first irrevocably fixed to take place. Let us bring this doctrine to the test of the Bible itself.

1. *Consider the doctrine as compared with the word of God in Jeremiah* xviii. 1-12. *The words of the prophet there are the words of God.* He writes as follows:—"The word which came to Jeremiah from the Lord, saying, Arise, and go down to the potter's house; and there I will cause thee to hear my words. Then I went down to the potter's house; and behold, He wrought a work on the wheels. And the vessel that He made of clay was marred in the hand of the potter: so He made it again another vessel, as seemed good to the potter to make it. Then the word of the Lord came to me, saying, O house of Israel, can not I do with you as this potter? saith the Lord. Behold, as the clay is in the potter's hand, so are ye in mine hand, O House of Israel. At what instant I shall speak

concerning a nation, and concerning a kingdom, to pluck up, and to pull down, and to destroy it; if that nation against whom I have pronounced turn from their evil, I will repent of the evil that I thought to do unto them. And at what instant I shall speak concerning a nation, and concerning a kingdom, to build, and to plant it; if it do evil in my sight, that it obey not my voice, then I will repent of the good wherewith I said I would benefit them. Now, therefore, go to, speak to the men of Judah, and to the inhabitants of Jerusalem, saying, Thus saith the Lord, Behold, I frame evil against you, and devise a device against you; return ye now every one from his evil way, and make your ways and your doings good. And they said, There is no hope; but we will walk after our own devices, and we will every one do the imagination of his evil heart."

It is most clear that the principle of this passage is perfectly irreconcilable with the doctrine that the condemnation of the lost is *fixed* from eternity. Only hear Jehovah as He puts the people upon the wheel of trial, as the potter does with the clay. Mark His words, as He speaks concerning a nation " to pluck up, and to pull down, and to destroy it." Does He speak as if the matter of condemnation were fixed irrevocably from eternity? Who can possibly admit such a *fixing* in the face of these words of God? Only think of its being known, as He used this remarkable parable, that every instance of condemnation that *could* take place, had been *fixed* from eternity! How would the parable have looked then? It is true that those who ascribe a secret will to God which differs from His revealed will, and who are *proud* to acknowledge that they can not *pretend* to reconcile the two—such may hold anything whatever; but how can any one, of sober sense and honesty of mind, believe that all this profession on the part of God was inconsistent with His own secret desire? and how could the scope and bearing of this passage be consistent with a decree ordaining certain men to certain death?

2. *Consider the doctrine before us along with the word of God in Ezekiel* xviii. 19-32—"Yet say ye, Why? doth not the son bear the iniquity of the father? When the son hath done that which is lawful and right, and hath kept all my statutes, and hath done them, he shall surely live. The soul that sinneth, it shall die. The son shall not bear the iniquity of the father, neither shall the father bear the iniquity of the son; the righteousness of the righteous shall be upon him, and the wickedness of the wicked shall be upon him. But if the wicked will turn from all his sins that he hath committed, and keep all my statutes, and do that which is lawful and right, he shall surely live, he shall not die. All his transgressions that he hath committed, they shall not be mentioned unto him; in his righteousness that he hath done, he shall live. Have I any pleasure at all that the wicked should die? saith the Lord God; and not that he should return from his ways, and live? But when the righteous turneth away from his righteousness, and committeth iniquity, and doeth according to all the abominations that the wicked man doeth, shall he live? All

his righteousness that he hath done shall not be mentioned; in his trespass that he hath trespassed, and in his sin that he hath sinned, in them shall he die. Yet ye say, The way of the Lord is not equal. Hear now, O house of Israel, Is not my way equal? are not your ways unequal? When a righteous man turneth away from his righteousness, and committeth iniquity, and dieth in them; for his iniquity that he hath done shall he die. Again, when the wicked man turneth away from his wickedness that he hath committed, and doeth that which is lawful and right, he shall save his soul alive. Because he considereth, and turneth away from all his transgressions that he hath committed, he shall surely live, he shall not die. Yet saith the house of Israel, The way of the Lord is not equal. O house of Israel, are not my ways equal? are not your ways unequal? Therefore I will judge you, O house of Israel, every one according to his ways, saith the Lord God. Repent, and turn yourselves from all your transgressions, so iniquity shall not be your ruin. Cast away from you all your transgressions, whereby you have transgressed; and make you a new heart, and a new spirit; for why will ye die, O house of Israel? For I have no pleasure in the death of him that dieth, saith the Lord God; wherefore turn yourselves and live ye."

Now, surely, if the idea of an eternal fixing of the death of the wicked were a truth, we may well ask, how can you imagine the force of *sincerity* as existing in that most solemn appeal of God? Only let us suppose the case of a man who should possess a thousand slaves, and he professes to govern them on principles of strictest equity. Well, he writes down the names of three hundred of them in a book, and writes over these his own unalterable decree that they shall live; and he writes down the seven hundred in another book, *determining unalterably* that they shall die. And having done so, he goes forth among his slaves, and gives utterance to such an appeal as that before us—What would you think of such a master? Would it better the case to suppose that his slaves were all criminals, and that he had a secret power by which he could easily turn the heart of the criminal, and without which that heart could not be turned,—that he had determined to carry out the decrees he had written, by giving and withholding this power? Does not the heart sicken at such a representation of *man*, and yet, how shall any one show the *feature* in which it is a misrepresentation of the idea formed of God, and solemnly stated in the confession of the majority of Scottish Christians? Hear, my hearer, the doctrine of eternally foreordained condemnation, and read, and ponder the words of God by Ezekiel, and see if you *can* believe them both. If you can, your faith may be wrong "in kind," but it is surely mighty in strength! No; we reject with indignation the idea that He who appealed to the fact that He was ready and most solicitous to alter the sentence of death, could have fixed that sentence by an eternal and unalterable decree.

3. *Consider the doctrine before us in connection with the appeal of God in Ezekiel* xxxiii. 1-20—
"Again the word of the Lord came unto me, saying, Son of man, speak to the children of thy peo-

ple, and say unto them, When I bring the sword upon a land, if the people of the land take a man of their coasts, and set him for their watchman—if, when he seeth the sword come upon the land, he blow the trumpet, and warn the people; then, whosoever heareth the sound of the trumpet, and taketh not warning; if the sword come and take him away, his blood shall be upon his own head. He heard the sound of the trumpet, and took not warning; his blood shall be upon him: but he that taketh warning shall deliver his soul. But if the watchman see the sword come, and blow not the trumpet, and the people be not warned; if the sword come, and take any person from among them, he is taken away in his iniquity; but his blood will I require at the watchman's hand. So thou, O son of man, I have set thee a watchman unto the house of Israel; therefore, thou shalt hear the word at my mouth, and warn them from me. When I say unto the wicked, O wicked man, thou shalt surely die; if thou dost not speak to warn the wicked from his way, that wicked man shall die in his iniquity; but his blood will I require at thine hand. Nevertheless, if thou warn the wicked of his way to turn from it; if he do not turn from his way, he shall die in his iniquity; but thou hast delivered thy soul. Therefore, O thou son of man, speak unto the house of Israel, Thus ye speak, saying, If our transgressions and our sins be upon us, and we pine away in them, how should we then live? Say unto them, As I live, saith the Lord God, I have no pleasure in the death of the wicked; but that the wicked turn from his way and live: turn ye, turn ye from your evil ways; for why will ye die, O house of Israel? Therefore, thou son of man, say unto the children of thy people, The righteousness of the righteous shall not deliver him in the day of his transgression; as for the wickedness of the wicked, he shall not fall thereby in the day that he turneth from his wickedness; neither shall the righteous be able to live for his righteousness in the day that he sinneth. When I shall say to the righteous, that he shall surely live; if he trust to his own righteousness, and commit iniquity, all his righteousness shall not be remembered; but for his iniquity that he hath committed, he shall die for it. Again, when I say unto the wicked, Thou shalt surely die; if he turn from his sin, and do that which is lawful and right; if the wicked restore the pledge, give again that he had robbed, walk in the statutes of life, without committing iniquity; he shall surely live, he shall not die. None of his sins that he hath committed, shall be mentioned unto him; he hath done that which is lawful and right, he shall surely live. Yet the children of thy people say, The way of the Lord is not equal; but as for them, their way is not equal. When the righteous turneth from his righteousness, and committeth iniquity, he shall even die thereby. But if the wicked turn from his wickedness, and do that which is lawful and right, he shall live thereby. Yet ye say, The way of the Lord is not equal. O ye house of Israel, I will judge you every one after his ways."

There are several points of immense moment in this passage. *First*, observe the appointment of the watchman. For what purpose is he appointed?

Is it not to *prevent* the death of those who are exposed to the sword? No doubt this is the design of his appointment. Is it, then, to *prevent* the fulfillment of a divine decree that he is placed on the watch-tower? But what is his crime? If the watchman fail to give warning, and the people of his charge perish—What is his crime? Is it that of not doing his utmost to prevent the accomplishment of an unalterable decree of God? If the doctrine before us be true, this is his crime. But passing from the watchman to his God,—On what principle are we to understand His most solemn protestation, that He has "NO PLEASURE in the death of the wicked?" Are we to hold that the accomplishment of that which He was *pleased* to ordain, is no pleasure to Him? How can you compare the doctrine of the Confession, and that of this passage, without seeing that they are perfect contradictions. To say that black is white is not more palpably a contradiction, than to say that God *pleased* to ordain the death of the wicked, and that He has no pleasure in that death! To pretend that there is "mystery" in such a case is just equivalent to the conduct of the man who should say that night is day; and when contradicted, he should shield himself by the wretched pretense that his words contained a mystery. He that should be imposed on by such a subterfuge, would be simple indeed. The only way in which I have seen it attempted to get rid of this difficulty otherwise, is, by holding that the "wicked" here are not to be taken for any but the *elect* wicked. Calvin says regarding Ezekiel xxxiii. 11 :—"If this be extended to all mankind, why does He not urge many to repentance, whose minds are more flexible to obedience than others who grow more and more callous to His daily invitations?"* And hence he goes deliberately to work to show, that it is only the elect wicked in whose death Jehovah has no pleasure. But such an attempt at evasion only renders matters worse, inasmuch as the whole force of the passage is directed to those who shall be judged according to their own ways. The Lord is speaking of those who shall "die in their iniquity," and hence, *can not* be speaking of the elect. We, then, most earnestly request the hearer to take up the doctrine supposed to be taught in the passage before us—lay it side by side with those passages of the Bible—study both most carefully—see if, doing your very best, you can bring them into a position in which they will not mutually condemn each other. See thus the pressing necessity for understanding the text before us on other principles.

Before proceeding to the text it may be well to notice in passing, a difficulty that arises in the mind in reading the passages I have now quoted. It is that of forgiveness and death being apparently suspended upon the penitence or impenitence of the sinner. It is that of the destiny of the sinner apparently *depending upon his works*, and not upon the atonement. To obviate this difficulty, the hearer has only to remember that the God who speaks in these passages is a *propitiated* judge, and thus He speaks upon the understanding of the atonement. The sacrifice was continually before the

* Institutes, b. iii.

minds of those to whom He addressed Himself; and it could not fail to be seen by them, that the pardon of the sinner on his turning from sin, was upon the ground and understanding of this atonement.

II. LET US NOW EXAMINE THE REAL MEANING OF THE TEXT CHIEFLY BEFORE US.

In order clearly to ascertain the real meaning and intention of the apostle in this verse, it is only necessary to examine its connection with those that follow it.

1. *What is the condemnation spoken of?* Jude says that the persons of whom he speaks " were before of old ordained to *this condemnation.*" It is most important that we understand the real bearing of these words. It is not difficult for the hearer to glance over the whole epistle, and see the only condemnation mentioned in it. You will see that it is the execution of judgment which God, as a Judge, inflicts upon the finally impenitent. In the fifth verse he speaks of the destruction of those in Egypt " *who believed not.*" In the sixth verse he speaks of the punishment of the angels who kept not their first estate. In the seventh verse he mentions the ruin of the people of Sodom and Gomorrah, as the vengeance of eternal fire. And in the fifteenth verse he describes the last judgment. All these verses lead us to one thing, and that is the final and eternal condemnation of the soul. Expositors are perfectly right in saying that this passage speaks of everlasting condemnation, and if it were

correctly expounded in its other parts as it is in this, their doctrine would have foundation.

2. *What is the nature of the foreordination here spoken of?* This leads us to the most important part of all; and I shall endeavor to answer the question, first, by showing the real meaning of the word used by Jude, and then by attending to his description of the foreordination of which he speaks. I remark, then, that the word here translated "before ordained," can not be applied to a secret decree. It has the meaning of a public proclamation, as one of its essential features. In proof of this I may quote some of those instances in which it occurs in the New Testament. Rom. xv. 4,—"For whatsoever things were *written aforetime*, were written for our learning." This phrase, "written aforetime," is the translation of the word in the text before us, rendered "before ordained." Now try to form the idea of the things written for universal learning being secret. Again, Gal. iii. 1—"Before whose eyes Jesus Christ *hath been evidently set forth*, crucified, among you." The words, "hath been evidently set forth," are the translation of the word translated in Jude, "*before ordained.*" Now try to form a conception of agreement between a thing being "evidently set forth," and its being *secretly* foreordained! can one word signify both of these? Why make such a monstrous difference in the rendering of a word? We can not but believe that the system which requires such translations is frail indeed.

We may now ask if the connection at all permits such a wide departure from the ordinary usage of language, as to render the word which usually signifies a public proclamation, by a " secret decree ? " This leads us to apply to the epistle, in order that we may see whether there is any public proscription mentioned. You find it in the fourteenth and fifteenth verses. "And Enoch also, the seventh from Adam, prophesied of them, saying, Behold the Lord cometh with ten thousand of His saints to execute judgment upon all, and to convince all that are ungodly among them of all their ungodly deeds," etc. Now here is a *proscription*, a public proclamation consigning all that are ungodly to condemnation. This is manifestly the proscription which was given of old, and to which the apostle refers. It is the proscription of *a class* bearing a certain specified character; and it is manifestly given for the purpose of warning all to leave that class, ere the day of final retribution come. This is just as different from a secret decree, fixing the condemnation of a certain portion of men from eternity, as infinite love is from the most inexplicable tyranny. And it is truly relieving to the soul to see that the Bible is most eminently consistent with itself. Let us take an illustration of the diversity between these two ideas:—Let us suppose a king whose power is absolute, and he has millions of subjects. He takes two immense rolls, and, in secret, he writes down one portion of his people in one, and another portion in the other roll. There, then, are the *names* of the people in two enormous lists. Over the one list he writes "LIFE," and over the other, "DEATH;" and fixes the destinies of each individual according to his pleasure! Well, suppose another king who has as many subjects, and he issues a very simple proclamation declaring the portion that he has provided for those who follow the will of their king, and another proclamation declaring the doom of those who persist in rebellion. He *proscribes* every rebel, but he does so *publicly ;* that all may flee from the ranks of rebellion. Is there not immense distance between the conduct of these two kings? Such is the distance between the usual view of the decree of God, and that really given by Jude. Even as early as Enoch, a public proclamation existed, declaring the doom of the ungodly. It was made MOST PUBLIC, and hence the perfect inexcusableness of those who still continued to be ungodly; because the moment they ceased to be ungodly persons, that moment they ceased to be proscribed persons.

III. CONSIDER PARTICULARLY THE SCRIPTURE TRUTH TAUGHT IN THIS PASSAGE.

That truth is of incalculable importance to those that are still without God.

1. *How remarkable the warning that wicked men have got!* Jude says that they were proscribed to condemnation *long ago*—aye, even so far back as the days of Enoch, the condemnation of the ungodly was *publicly proclaimed to the world.* Every succeeding age has not only had the opportunity of reading this proscription, but has also had its own particular proscription of the ungodly. Thus has Jehovah been keeping the warning truth before the eyes of men, in a man-

ner more powerful than if He had written it on the sky; and thus has He shown His own deep desire that they should flee from the ranks of the condemned. O! my hearer, if you are still ungodly do not forget that you are so, in the very face of Jehovah's public proclamation, that the wages of sin is death. Do not forget that you are keeping over your own head His fearful threatening, by keeping yourself among those who have been the condemned from the beginning of the world.

2. *How inexcusable the continued ungodliness of those who live at the present time!* They have the experience of the world, and the teaching and warning of God during all generations, coming upon them in combined energy, and yet they go on to the fatal hour of judgment in the face of all. It was folly to resist the truth, even when Enoch spake; how much more so now? Innumerable souls have perished since then,—innumerable instances have demonstrated the certainty of the ruin to the ungodly; and all these are before the eyes of those who are ungodly now! O! how will the soul, that passes unprepared to the judgment from this age, be able to look up at all? How will any one be able to answer the fearful question,—How could you remain ungodly in defiance of the voice of so many ages, and that but the descending echo of the voice of God? My hearer, be warned in time. As yet your soul is as free to the love of God as if you had never sinned. No unalterable decree hinders your present and eternal safety;— nothing can hinder it but your own will. Jehovah

is waiting for you—longing for you—pleading for you to be reconciled; and the united warning of all the warning truth that has been delivered to mankind, is used to urge you to flee from the wrath to come.

LECTURE XIV.

PREDESTINATION AND THE BOOK OF LIFE.

The words of Scripture which we are called to consider in this lecture, are found in Rev. xvii. 8—" And they who dwell on the earth shall wonder (whose names were not written in the book of life from the foundation of the world.)" This is a prediction having reference to a great coming delusion; and the declaration is, that those whose names were not written in the book of life from the foundation of the world, shall be carried away with the delusion, and shall " worship" (chap. xiii. 8) the great deceiver of men. It is not our business at present to say what particular delusion this is; but to take up the description given of those who are to be led off by the deceiver. The doctrine of "*preterition*," as it is called, or of God's " passing by" millions of men and leaving them out of His decree of life, is supposed to be contained here; and it is with this aspect of the doctrine of reprobation that we have to do in considering this passage. The nature of the doctrine itself, is stated thus—" God, by an eternal and immutable decree, out of His mere love, for the praise of His glorious grace, to be manifested in due time, hath elected some angels to glory; and in Christ hath chosen some men to life, and the means thereof; and also, according to His sovereign power, and the unsearchable counsel of His own will (whereby He extendeth or withholdeth favor as He pleaseth), hath *passed by* and foreordained the rest to dishonor and wrath, to be for their sin inflicted to the praise of His glorious justice."* In explaining this doctrine, an author of the most extensive, and still mighty influence in Scotland, says of the reprobate, that God " did not write their names in the book of life, or mark them out for His sheep, people, and subjects, and objects, and vessels of mercy; and, in consequence hereof, determined to withhold from them the undeserved favor of redemption and reconciliation through Christ, and of effectual calling, justification, adoption, faith, and holiness."† Such, then, is the sentiment supposed to be the doctrine of the passage before us, for it is quoted as a proof, by this same author, that God has from eternity written the names of the smaller number " of men in the book of life." The idea is clearly this—that there is a book of life—that certain names have been written there from eternity—that certain others have been left out from eternity—that the list has been thus eternally complete—none can be added to it, and none taken away. Now, this is the doctrine which we require to consider in connection with the passage before us.

I. Let us consider some scriptural objections to this doctrine.

By these we shall be enabled to perceive the real

---

* Larger Catechism, Q. 13th.
† Brown's Dict. Decree.

meaning of the passage much more definitely than otherwise.

1. *The doctrine in question is utterly inconsistent with the threatening of God to blot the name of the sinner out of the book of life.* It is, indeed, the very foundation of the doctrine, that blotting out of that book is absolutely impossible; just as the insertion of any name not now in it is also impossible. How, then, does this agree with the following passages of Scripture. Exodus xxxii. 31-33—" And Moses returned unto the Lord, and said, Oh! this people have sinned a great sin, and have made them gods of gold. Yet now, if thou wilt forgive their sin: and if not, blot me, I pray thee, out of thy book which thou hast written." And the Lord said unto Moses, " Whosoever hath sinned against me, *him will I blot out of my book.*" Is it possible to believe that the names were written in the book here spoken of by an unalterable decree? God says, "*I will blot out of my book.*" Who shall reply to God, "*It is impossible?*" Who shall declare that to be unalterable which He says *is alterable*, and which He declares He will alter? But we have a statement of still greater effect in Rev. iii. 5. Here Jesus says, " He that overcometh shall be clothed in white raiment, and *I will not blot out his name out of the book of life,* but I will confess his name before my Father, and before His angels." Now Jesus must have been here speaking of a real blessing, not of an imaginary one; and if it were true, that no name *could possibly* be blotted out of the book of life, what is the real force of His words? Simply that He would not do that which is impossi-

ble. If the names in the book of life, are the names of those predestinated by an unalterable decree to stand there, it is impossible either to understand the threatening to Moses, or the promise here given, as of any force whatever. To make this fully clear, suppose that you have six servants, and that you write down three of their names in a book, with the *unalterable* determination of keeping these three, and dismissing the rest; will you ever think of threatening, or promising anything, as to blotting out, or not blotting out of these names? If you do, it can not be in sincerity; simply because it can not be according to truth. The threatening to blot out, involves and conveys to those that hear it, the *alterableness* of the list; and if the list is unalterable, the threatening is virtually a falsehood. I insist, therefore, that it is impossible to believe the doctrine before us, and also to recognize the sincerity of God in the passages quoted. But these are not all. Rev. xxii. 19, is fully as much to the point as either of those quoted. There John says—"And if any man shall take away from the words of the prophecy of this book, God shall take away his part out of the book of life, and out of the holy city, and from the things which are written in this book." Surely, we must regard this as a real threatening. Or are we to regard it in the light of the universal demonstration of love spoken of by a popular preacher, and already quoted? Must we have recourse to the notion that it is a threatening, "names and numbers being suppressed," but that it ceases to be so the moment the names are revealed? We take our stand upon the very first principles of truth and reason, and Scripture too, when we say that there can be no such threatenings with God. The very thought is infamous. It ought to be sufficient to sink for ever the reputation of the system that gives it birth and nourishment. Take, then, the threatening of God as *real*, and He declares that He will take the part of the man, who takes away from this book, out of the book of life. We have, then, most unquestionable ground for rejecting the idea, that the book of life is the list of the eternally predestinated. Such a doctrine *can not* stand the test of the threatenings and promises to which we have now referred.

2. *The doctrine that all the names written in the book of life were there from eternity, and by Jehovah's pleasure and decree, is utterly inconsistent with the punishment assigned for the crime of not being found there.* It is surely impossible for any one to suppose that God will punish a man eternally, for not having his name in His eternal decree of salvation. In Rev. xx. 14, 15, we have the following words: "And death and hell were cast into the lake of fire. This is the second death. And *whosoever was not found written in the book of life*, was cast into the lake of fire." Here, then, we are told, that the reason why men are at last cast into eternal fire, is, that their names are not written in the book of life. The one only crime mentioned, as fitting them for eternal death, is this,—their names are not in this book. This is the sum of all their guilt, and the cause of their perishing for ever. Now are you, my hearer, prepared to believe that Jehovah will cast men into eternal fire, because

their names are not found where they never were, and where it was no more possible for them to place them, than it is possible for man to reverse the decrees of God? If, according to the doctrine before us, these men had no conceivable control over their names being there or not, then CAN you believe that they perish eternally because their names are not in that book? Try to reconcile these two doctrines,—that God above can put a name in the book of life or keep it there, and yet that men will be cast into hell, because their names are not found in that eternal roll. You may attempt the reconciliation, but with what success? You may shroud it in the idea of "mystery;" but the "mystery" is only too shallow, or too clear, as it can not hide the horrid deformity of the doctrine of sending men to eternal hell for not having their names in an eternal decree. You may speak of "incomprehensibles" —Alas! this doctrine is only too easily comprehended. The idea that God should eternally punish men for not setting down their names in His book an eternity before they were born, is certainly not a wide idea; it is narrow, and most unlike that unfathomable love that gave the Son of God to die for a whole world. It is comprehensible as a horrid absurdity, and that only.

3. *It is entirely an assumed matter that this book of life existed before men existed.* You will observe that it is not said from *before* the foundation of the world. It is only *from* the foundation of the world. There is no ground here for supposing that there was a book of life for men before men lived. We have yet to see what the book of life is,

and *when* the list in it began to be filled up, and purged of those requiring to be blotted out of it; but it is *most* important to observe, and to *reflect* upon the observation, that the whole fabric of the doctrine of an eternal book of life, rests upon a perfectly gratuitous assumption. Try, my hearer, to find out one word, in the text now before us, to warrant the idea of the existence of this list of names before men existed, and your utmost effort will not furnish you with one. Now it is too bad to found a doctrine, and, in defense of it, to ask men to accept, on pain of perdition itself, the most gross inconsistencies, when all the ground upon which you lay a foundation-stone, is simply—NOTHING. A doctrine that calls so loudly upon us as to demand the laying aside of our common sense, and the reason which God has mercifully spared to us, should have some firmer ground. "*From* or *since* the foundation of the world"—must mean "from eternity!" If it can not, then where is the foundation for the story of an eternal book of life? Where? Where? Will muttering mystery answer? No. It must leave the echo to answer only—"*where?*" O! it is impossible to speak in terms too strong in view of thousands groping in the darkness of uncertainty, trying in vain to read their names in the book of life—kept in this darkness by a doctrine that has no better ground to rest upon, than the assertions of its advocates. It is pitiful to think of men casting off Christianity, because that holy truth has been *masked*, by pretended friends, with this fearful doctrine of predestination; when any one might have the doctrine sent to the winds by only asking for, and sifting its pretended scriptural authority.

II. LET US NOW CONSIDER THE REAL MEANING OF THIS PASSAGE REGARDING THE BOOK OF LIFE.

Having endeavored to remove the rubbish, we are better prepared to see the beauty of truth, and to feel its warning and cheering power.

1. *The book of life is the list of the living.* What other idea can we form from the words before us in the text, than just that of a list of those who now are living, and distinguished from those who are dead. There are two lists—the one of the living, the other of the dead, and the book before us is the list of the living. It is the list of those who are not, while in that list, as yet consigned to death. This idea of the book of life, or of the scroll of the living, is the only definite idea that we can form in accordance with those passages of Scripture which we have been called to notice. This idea agrees with the words of God to Moses; when He said, "Him that hath sinned against me will I blot out of my book," He manifestly uttered the same sentiment as that which He uttered when He said—"The soul that sinneth it shall die." The soul is regarded as living, and as yet among the living, and its name in the list of the living; but the threatening is, that sinning, it shall die, and thus be blotted from the list of those that live. In the sixty-ninth Psalm, we have an idea exactly the same as that before us, and such as shows us the meaning of the book of life, verse 25—" Let them

be blotted out of the book of the living, and not be written with the righteous." Here it is manifest that the Psalmist regards the book of the living as simply the number of those who are not consigned to death, but who, because of their fearful guilt, would yet be so. He has no notion of an unchangeable list, from which no one can be subtracted, and to which none can be added. Far less could he have the idea of two lists, one consisting of those doomed to death before they were born, and another of those predestinated to life. The book of life here stands before us in the persons of living men, not yet consigned to death by the God who made them.

2. *It must be plain that this has been a list ever since man was created.* Ever since there were living beings, there was a list of the living—a scroll of life, from which it was possible that names might be blotted out by the sentence of a righteous God. The Psalmist leads us by a two-fold expression to see whose names were allowed to stand on this book, and whose were struck out. He says—" written with *the righteous.*" These were the class whose names remained in the book of life—"the wicked" were struck from it. But this leads us to a much more clear idea still, inasmuch as it leads us to the question—Who are "*righteous*" in the sight of God? The answer is, those only who have not sinned, and those who appear in the robe of righteousness of Jesus. No human being can stand as the *living,* or on the list of life, in the sight of God, who is not standing on the ground of the Saviour's sacrifice. Hence, this book of life is expressly call-

ed the book of life of the slain Lamb. (Rev. xiii. 8.) Those written in this book, therefore, are those who stand in a position of safety and life, through the death of Jesus. They are the list of the living who *live* because He *died for them*. Those that are blotted out from this list, are those who reject the atonement of Jesus, and choose to meet Jehovah on the ground of their own works, or to bid Him defiance by their continued sin. The figure, therefore, of a scroll of names, and of the blotting out of names from this list of the living, is one of great force, and such as sends home its warning power to every heart. O! my hearer, is your name among the list of those who live by the blood of the Lamb? Or have you good reason to think that you are blotted out of that list, and "condemned already." This is the question of questions for you. Let it not be evaded.

3. *Let us now consider whose names have been at least once in this book of life.* The usual idea of a certain number being written here from all eternity by the decree of God, and of the rest being left out, is, we have seen, wrong. And we shall see, from many considerations, that every man's name has been at least *once* in this book of life. It will now be generally granted that those dying in infancy are saved—that *all such* are saved—that so far as the sin of the first Adam affects them for evil, the atonement of the second Adam proves their remedy, and hence as those who have never had it in their power to reject the Saviour, they live for ever through Him.* This may be dis-

* Dr. Russell on Infant Salvation.

puted, but it can not be overturned. Now, seeing that an infant dying in infancy is safe, and rises from the grave because of the resurrection of Jesus, just as it died in consequence of the sin of Adam; must not that infant have been born to stand upon the list of the living, and that the list too of the slain Lamb? But if we apply, as we must, this principle to those infants that die, on what ground can we withhold it from those that live? They are born in every respect on the same footing; and the idea that God, who is no respecter of persons, will bring an infant into the world decreed to live for ever, and another decreed to die for ever, is simply, as we have already fully seen, an infamous libel on His holy character. Here, then, we have it clear before us, that all men are born upon the list of life of the Lamb slain. Yes, my hearer, you were once an infant; and, had you died then, you would have opened your immortal eyes in glory; and your first sight would have been Jesus your Saviour, and best friend. Then you stood in the list of the saved and living—your name was upon the book of life. *Where is it now?* As an infant you stood before God on the ground of the work of Jesus, for you had not been born but for that work—now that you are an intelligent and free creature, have you renounced, or willfully refrained from taking that ground? Then dream not of your name being in the book of life.

4. *Consider now what it is that takes a man's name from this book of life.* "He that believeth hath everlasting life;" and, consequently, his name must stand on the list of the living, and that the

list of the slain Lamb. "*He that believeth not is condemned already*," and can his name be on that list? It is impossible. The condemned man is struck from the book of the living by the sentence of death being passed upon him. Think, then, my hearer, of being "condemned *already*," and see if it be possible to conceive of the name of him, who is condemned already, standing upon the list of those who have eternal life. But when does his name cease to be among the living? He is condemned already, "*because* he has not believed on the only-begotten Son of God." It is the *refusal* to credit the gospel, and the *rejection* of Jesus, that strike the name from the list of the living. The moment you become capable of receiving Jesus as the ground of acceptance with God, and in the sight of Jehovah *refuse* Him, and take your stand upon other ground, you are condemned. Your name that in infancy stood on the book of life, ceases to be there any longer. You are numbered with transgressors. You are condemned. You are "dead" by the sentence of your God. The name of an unbeliever is not found in the book of life. It would be absurdity to say to any there, they are "condemned," or that, "the wrath of God abideth on them." We see, then, clearly, what it is that takes a name from the Lamb's book of life. O! my hearer, this is a different doctrine from the idea that you have no control upon your name being in that book, or out of it. If your name is not there, *you have taken it out.* It is by your own act that you stand among the condemned.

5. *Consider, then, what class of men are before*

us in the passage chiefly under notice. It is most manifestly as *a class of character* that they are named—it is as those who, having refused to believe on Jesus, are exposed to the power of the deceiver. The difficulty connected with the text, is the same as that connected with a passage which we have already considered. It is the difficulty arising from looking to the persons spoken of as *individuals* and not *as a class:* "Who were before of old ordained to this condemnation." This at once leads the mind to fancy that the *individuals* immediately before us were proscribed before they were born; whereas, when we read the proscription itself, as written by Enoch, we see that it was the CLASS, and not particular individuals that were proscribed, and that so soon as an individual ceased to belong to the class, he ceased to be affected by the proscription, or to be alluded to in the mention of it; and so soon as an individual entered the class, the proscription then affected and included him. So is it in the case before us. Rejecters of Jesus, *as a class*, have not been found in the book of life since the foundation of the world. This applies to no man unless as an unbeliever. The moment he ceases from rejecting Jesus, he ceases to be alluded to in the statement. It has no application to infants. These have been written in that book ever since it was in existence and they together. But the moment a human being passes from this class, without believing in Jesus and in Jehovah as a propitiated God, he passes from the class whose names are in the book of life; and the moment that he ceases to belong to the condemned class, by receiving Jesus as the ground of his acceptance with God, the declaration of the text ceases from including him. Every other view of this passage will be found to involve absurdity, and nothing can be clearer than that as this is the view that must be taken of the proscription, so it is that which must be taken of the book of life.

6. *We see now, in conclusion, who they are that "wonder" at, and "worship" delusion.* They are not some poor unfortunates whose names were left out of the purpose of God in eternity, and who could no more help this than they could have created the world before they had existed; but they are those who have rejected the slain Lamb, and who in rejecting Him, have taken their names and their part from the book of life. It is the absence of Jesus from the mind that ever exposes it to delusion. It is the want of the anchor of the soul, that leaves it to be tossed upon every passing wave, and driven before every passing wind. Most powerfully, then, does this argue the necessity of believing in Jesus. Most clearly does it show, that all are welcome to enter among the saved. All are welcome to believe in Jesus. O! my hearer, try this, as not only peace to the soul, but as an effectual bar to every error that can enter your mind; you will find that the soul that is safe in the possession of the Lamb slain, is safe indeed. Millions of delusions may present themselves, or be presented to the soul, but if that soul is *full* of the glory of Jesus, they are presented in vain. Thus, among the list of those whose life is a life of faith on the Son of God, temptation will fall powerless upon your preoccupied mind.

LECTURE XV.

PREDESTINATION AS FOUND IN THE BIBLE.

IN this lecture, our attention will be directed chiefly to Ephesians i. 5—"*Having predestinated us to the adoption of children by Jesus Christ to Himself, according to the good pleasure of His will.*" We shall also consider in connection with this, the only other passages in which predestination is mentioned in the Bible, as applicable to men themselves. Rom. viii. 29, 30, and Eph. i. 11. The examination of these passages together, will enable us to see the whole Scripture doctrine of the predestination of men.

Before proceeding to examine the real meaning of these passages, however, it may be well to remove the vail that has been cast upon them by those who have borrowed Bible words to designate a doctrine the very opposite of Bible truth. The following is the plain broad statement of the doctrine of predestination supposed by Calvin to be taught in these, and kindred passages: "Predestination," he says, " we call the eternal decree of God, by which He hath determined in Himself what He would have to become of every individual of mankind. For they are not all created with a similar destiny, but eternal life is foreordained for some, and eternal damnation for others. Every man, therefore, being created for one or other of these ends, we say, he is predestinated either to life or to death."* This is as clear and honest a statement of the most fearful of doctrines, as could possibly be desired, and its clearness enables us to meet it much more easily and certainly by a most distinct denial from the Word of God itself. You will see clearly that, according to this doctrine, men are created in a predestinated condition to life or death.

I. LET US CONSIDER SOME REASONS FOR REFUSING TO REGARD THIS DOCTRINE AS THAT TAUGHT IN THE PASSAGES BEFORE US.

These reasons will be found to be such as to render it impossible to regard the doctrine of those passages, and that which we have quoted, as the same.

1. *The persons spoken of in Romans* viii. 29, 30, *are those who love God.* This is seen most undeniably from the 28th verse—" And we know that all things work together for good to *those that love God*, to them who are the called according to His purpose." This is the character given of those who are said to be predestinated. Now, how can we apply this character to those who are yet without God, and lying in wickedness. According to the doctrine in question, those now in an ungodly state, who shall be saved at some future time, are predestinated. How can this be inferred from the predestination of those who love God? The Bible speaks of those who bear this character, and of *such only*,

* Calvin's Inst., book iii. chap. xxiv.

as predestinated—how can any man infer from this that others who have *no* love to God, but hate Him, are predestinated also?

2. *Further, those who are spoken of as predestined by Paul, are declared to be justified.* "Who shall lay anything to the charge of God's elect? It is God that justifieth, who is he that condemneth?" Such is the state of those whom Paul says are predestinated. Is this the state of all that shall be saved? Are they all *justified?* Are we to believe in the monster absurdity of *eternal* justification? Can no one lay anything to the charge of those who are "the children of wrath even as others," and on whom "the wrath of God" is said to abide? No one can doubt that many will yet believe who are now unbelievers, and thus many who are condemned now will yet be justified; but are we to believe that all such are now justified? Most assuredly not. Since, then, Paul declares regarding those that are elect and predestinated, that they are justified, does he not contradict the doctrine in question out and out? We can not see how on such a passage as this it is at all possible to found the doctrine of the predestination of unbelievers to life. The very least that can be said is, that there is no foundation for such a doctrine there.

3. *Those of whom Paul is speaking as predestinated, in his epistle to the Ephesians, are "saints and faithful in Christ Jesus."* Now the important question is, How can you infer the predestination of those who are yet "lying in wickedness" from the statement that those are predestinated who are "saints and believers in Jesus?" It is quite

true that these holy believers are predestinated, but does this imply either that they always were so, or that others, who are under the wrath of God, as rebels still, are now so? The believers were justified when Paul wrote to them. Can we infer from this, either that they were always so or that others yet in unbelief are justified? Mark again, my hearer, the *nothingness* of the ground upon which this doctrine rests. Where in the Word of God do you read of the predestination of those who are yet unborn, or still in unbelief? The doctrine of the predestination of such has no more ground in these passages than has the sanctification of those yet in unbelief. If you hold the one from these statements, you may just as well hold the other. Surely, this is some reason for regarding these passages as entirely free from the charge of that fearful doctrine.

4. *Still further, those said to be predestinated are also said to be " accepted in the beloved."* Are we, then, to hold that they were always " accepted in the beloved?" They were the "children of wrath"—were they, then, "accepted in the beloved?" Now, if we must not think, because they are now accepted, that they were always so, how are we to believe that they were always predestinated, because Paul says that they were so when he wrote? Is it not as clear as truth can be that these passages DO NOT TEACH an eternal predestination of these persons, far less do they teach the eternal predestination of others who are yet without God and without hope in the world. How singular it is, that so many should accept that giant

error, that men are eternally predestinated to life and death, as if it were taught in these passages of the Word of God! The word "predestinate" is quite sufficient by its mere *sound* to call up the ideas of an irresistible decree of life and death, and yet no such decree is found connected with the word in the Book of God.

This line of argument might be lengthened out to any extent; for anything imaginable is just as really said in these passages as that these persons were always predestinated, or that others yet in sin are predestinated along with them. If, therefore, any man will hold that these persons were always predestinated, and that others, still in unbelief when Paul wrote, were then predestinated to "the adoption"—we ask him kindly, but very firmly, to show us his authority from the Word of God. If he will have us to swallow that hideous idea, of beings created in a state of predestination to death, he is bound to give us the *strongest* ground for his demand; and if he does not furnish such ground, we charge him at once with groundlessly calumniating his God; and we demand, in the name of that God, that he retract the calumny, and do his utmost to undo the evil which he has effected by giving it the currency he has given it. O! let it not be thought a light matter to trifle with the name of the Lord. Let not his mind rise with self-sufficient pride who groundlessly lays the doctrine of eternal predestination, as we have quoted it, at Jehovah's door.

II. Let us now endeavor to see the real meaning and intention of the passages before us.

We have seen that no ground is afforded by these Scriptures for believing that those alluded to in them were predestinated from eternity; and still less, if possible, is there ground for believing that persons bearing a totally opposite character are *predestinated at all.* Our question now is, what predestination do they teach?

1. *What are we to understand by "the adoption" spoken of?* The answer to this question is of the very greatest moment. The idea usually is, that men are predestinated to undergo *regeneration.* Now, in not one of the texts under consideration is such an idea taught. They are believed to be predestinated to the enjoyment of "a special influence" on the one hand, and to be left without such influence on the other. No such idea is alluded to in these texts. The saints and faithful in Christ Jesus are, in the passage more especially under notice, said to be predestinated to "*the adoption.*" And when we ask, What adoption? we have the undoubted words of Paul himself in reply: Romans viii. 23, "Even we ourselves groan within ourselves, waiting for THE ADOPTION, *to wit*, THE REDEMPTION OF OUR BODY." Now, the word here rendered "the adoption" is the very same expanded into "the adoption of children" in Eph. i. 5. The blessing is manifestly the same, and it is explained in these words, "*the redemption of our body.*" No answer can be more direct and scrip-

tural than this, and it is confirmed by the expression, " predestinated to be conformed to the image of His Son," and by the whole connection of both passages. The truth taught, then, is, that those " saints and faithful in Christ Jesus " were predestinated to " the adoption, to wit, the redemption of their bodies," and so to be conformed to the glorious image of the glorified Jesus. This is the ONLY PREDESTINATION taught in these passages; and the task of making them teach the predestination of uncounted millions partly to heaven and partly to hell, or the predestination of some to be converted, is most hopeless indeed. Let me exhort the hearer to *think* over the passages and their connection, and see if it be possible to find the fearful ideas which we have quoted at the outset in any portion of them. No; but you do find that which is most cheering to the believer—that he is predestinated to stand in the glorified body of the resurrection, and to share the glory of his blessed Lord. This is the doctrine of predestination as taught in the Bible.

2. *We may notice shortly who are the persons predestinated to this glorious resurrection.* This we have in a great measure anticipated. Still it is important to give line upon line where, above all, error is apt to force itself in. Now it is impossible to point out the *line* or *word* in these passages by which countenance is given to the idea of those being predestinated to "the adoption," who are yet in their sins. Try again, my hearer, to find that line in which this notion has countenance. If you do hold that such are predestinated, then the bur-

den of proof lies with you. Prove it. We do see that those who love God are predestinated to "the adoption;" but does this argue that those who hate Him are so? Above all, does this argue that *others are predestinated to death?* No. The persons who are predestinated to the glory of the resurrection are those who are "*in Christ*," and *those alone*—those who are "accepted in the beloved," *and those alone.* In this very connection, it is declared that "if any man have not the Spirit of Christ, *he is none of His.*" The predestination of the Bible, then, is the predestination of those *already actually accepted* of God through Jesus, and of such alone, to the glory of the resurrection. Let that doctrine stand side by side with the words of the author we have quoted, and how vast the contrast between them! The one is cheering as the morning sun rising upon the departing night—the other is the horrid thunder cloud brooding over the masses of men in dire uncertainty as to who is to die by its deadly bolt. O! well may the heart pant for the rescue of men from that death-like spell that binds them so long to so gloomy a system!

3. *When does this predestination take place?* This question is virtually answered by what has been already said. Seeing that *only* believers and those who love God are "predestinated to the adoption," it is most clear that this act of predestination can not be regarded as having taken place until they believe and bear this character. Nor is there any more difficulty in believing this, than there is in believing that their justification can not take place until they believe. The one is the act of God

as really as the other; and if we can regard Him as justifying in time, so can we regard Him as predestinating to glory. The reason why the mind is misled on this point is, that the predestination of the persons spoken of, is supposed to have been fulfilled in their conversion, whereas it is only to be fulfilled in "*the redemption of their body.*" If any one should say that this predestination has been from eternity, let him quote his authority; and if he can not do this, let him show how a holy God can predestinate an *unbelieving* soul to glory; and if he can not do either, then let him acknowledge that he has derived his views of this doctrine from a teacher differing in his views from the Book of God.

There is greater importance in this view, of a predestination taking place *in time*, than may at first sight appear. How else, my hearer, can you intelligently believe that *you* may be predestinated to the glory of the resurrection? How, if still unbelieving, can you see your way into the lists of the predestinated? O! it is vastly momentous to know and feel assured that all the blessings of God's children are open to you, and to all. Eternal predestination shuts up the possibility of this assurance, and hides the welcome of a predestinating God from the sinner's anxious eye. Do not, then, sit lightly by the doctrine that a soul can only be predestinated to be conformed to the image of Jesus, *when*, by believing in Him, that soul becomes one of His. Then, and *not till then*, does He predestinate that soul for glory, just as then, and *not till then*, He frees that soul from condemnation.

4. *Let us notice the cause of this predestination of the believer to glory.* It is said to be the " good pleasure of His will." What is this but His benevolence?—benevolence is just good-willing—pleasing to do good. This is the characteristic of a benevolent heart. The cause, then, of any sinner being predestinated to glory is just the free sovereign grace or love of God. Some can not see that we ascribe predestination to the sovereign grace of God, unless we make it eternal, and hence they call the horrid doctrine of reprobation itself, " a doctrine of grace." But how is it that justification is of sovereign grace, and yet that it is not eternal? Surely, if the one may be of free sovereign grace, and yet take place in time, so may the other. Now, the question is clearly settled that the predestination spoken of in the Bible, like the justification spoken of there, does take place in time, and that both are of pure sovereign grace,—both according to the good pleasure of Jehovah's will. For a full view of the love that is manifested in predestination, we must look back into eternity, for it has been " *everlasting love* "—just as one must look forward to eternity, for it shall be "everlasting love;" but we have just the same thing to do in taking a full view of the love that justifies and pardons or accepts the guilty sinner on his believing in Jesus. There can be no greater difficulty in regarding predestination in time as according to the good pleasure of the will of God, than there is in regarding justification or pardon in time, as from the same source. To pass, then, from the controversial aspect of this truth, look to it in its own loveliness.

Here is a rebel—a traitor—a child of wrath, and an heir of hell: he does not seek God, but God seeks him, and follows him, step by step of his mad career, in the exercise of a forbearance which none but God could show. At length He gains the ear of the guilty wretch, and the sinful soul is arrested, convicted, and self-condemned. But the ransom has been paid, and the God of love "takes of the things which are Christ's," and shows them to the sinner. God assures the rebel, that though his sins are as scarlet, they shall be as white as snow; and when the unworthy and self-ejected outcast perceives his Father's love still full and free to him, and consents to be His restored child, then Jehovah not only pardons, justifies, and accepts, but also predestinates that man to "the adoption, to wit, the redemption of the body," and consequent glory of Jesus. All this must be from the "good pleasure of His will," for there is no other existing cause to account for it. O! my fellow-sinner, do not forget, if you are still refusing God, that according to "the good pleasure of His will," He is still following you as the most loving of fathers follows a prodigal. From the same cause He assures you, on oath, that He has no pleasure in your death, and beseeches you to turn and live; and from the same cause is He willing, nay, deeply earnest to forgive you—to justify you—to accept you as His child, and to *predestinate you* to eternal glory, that in your body and soul in heaven, you may be one of the "many brethren," among whom Jesus is the first-born. Be assured of this, if God's word can assure you. It is before you in your own tongue, that you may read it in the unfathomable depths of divine love, and know that that love is to you and to all your fellow-men.

5. *We may notice now on whose account men are predestinated to be conformed to the image of Jesus.* It is said, in the passage before us, that it is "through," or, literally, "on account of" Jesus Christ. It is remarkable that they are not said to be predestinated to Jesus—or, in order to be given to Him in due time—or, to be converted to His truth in due season;—they are predestinated on His account to "the adoption, to wit, the redemption of the body," and so to all the glories of eternal heaven. Here, then, the predestination of the believer is spoken of just as any other blessing given to him on believing. He is justified on account of Jesus; he has peace with God on the same account: and has been predestinated to future glory on the same account also. All this is simple and plain, ay, and mightily attractive to the soul of the outcast, who is assured of being now welcome to all this inestimable blessing and glory, "ON ACCOUNT OF JESUS CHRIST." He has no "account" of his own. He can not say, "accept of me, and predestinate me to to glory, and put it to my account." He is not only "without money and without a price" to give, but he has no credit with God. Blessed, then, be He who has welcomed us to "come, buy wine and milk," and have our names enrolled as the predestinated to glory "on His account." Surely, my unconverted, and, it may be, desponding hearer, there is grace enough here, and room enough in that grace for you. Can you present the plea of

Jesus' death and finished work in vain? Will God refuse to acknowledge His own Son's ransom, when you, though the vilest of the vile, present it as all your ransom why you should be justified in His sight and predestinated to eternal glory? Most assuredly not. Come, then, near to your Father. Do not think that any bar exists to your meeting Him in peace. Take up the guilty's only argument —THE RANSOM—the ransom PAID, and on account of Jesus be predestinated to everlasting joy.

6. *We may now notice, in closing, the object which God had in view in predestinating the believers of whom Paul spake.* This appears in the phrase "to Himself," or, "for His own sake." His grand object in this predestination of His restored prodigals is to give demonstration to the whole universe of His own faithfulness and honor. It also appears in the further statement—"To the praise of His glorious grace." This leads us forward to the time when Jesus and a company "which no man can number," shall stand forth before the universe clothed in unfading and eternal glory. Throughout the intelligent hosts of Jehovah's creation, this will constitute a theme of holy joy and deepest adoration. Truly it will be to the praise of His glorious grace, when "the adoption" has thus come and the wonderful work of salvation has reached its consummation.

O! my hearer, are you yet predestinated to this blessed end? Do not say that you "can not know" whether you are or not. Jehovah's predestination is no such secret or inscrutable thing as to be beyond your reach in your own case. You know if you are at peace with Him through our Lord Jesus Christ. You know if you stand before Him as your judge and king, on the ground that Jesus died for you. It is impossible to be in any difficulty as to this. And hence it is impossible to be in any great difficulty in determining what is your real situation in His sight. It is most clearly stated in the passage before us that the predestination "is on account of Jesus Christ." Are you, then, dealing with God on account of Jesus. Is He all your plea? If not, why may He not become so now? He died for you. His death is accepted as a sufficient answer for all your sins. Jehovah is ready to justify you. O! then agree with Him. Be one of His children now according to His own earnest request, and thus be predestinated with all those who believe.

LECTURE XVI.

PREDESTINATION AND THE SECURITY OF BELIEVERS.

THE text to which we direct attention in this lecture is 1 Thess. v. 9 :—" For God hath not appointed us to wrath, but to obtain salvation by our Lord Jesus Christ." This passage is supposed to teach that the feeling of security which the believer enjoys, arises from the knowledge of his being from eternity predestinated to life, while others have been appointed to wrath. It is quoted as proof of the doctrine of eternal preappointment to faith, both by the Westminster Confession and also by Brown in his Dictionary of the Bible. It is also looked upon by many as most unquestionably and clearly teaching the doctrine of predestination both to life and to death. Seeing that such is the case, and that Paul evidently regarded the truth stated here as one of great importance, our duty is plain, and we must examine the passage thoroughly. We shall see that the consolation was far better (and that in many respects) than any that could be derived from an eternal decree such as we have repeatedly quoted, while, at the same time, it bore upon its very face this most blessed mark of saving truth—it was a consolation free to every man. We shall consider the passage under two general divisions, first, as to its meaning, and second, as to its use.

I. Let us consider the meaning of the Apostle in this verse.

He is supposed to teach the eternal appointment of one portion of men to an eternal heaven, and the rest to an eternal woe. It will not be difficult to show that this is not the appointment spoken of by Paul, and that the one he spoke of is of a very different character indeed.

1. *The word here translated "appointed" never means preappointment.* It is most important to mark this, though I have already noticed it in the course of these lectures. The word signifies literally "*placed,*" or "*set,*" and never "*preappointed*" in any one instance in which it occurs. It will make this more clear to the mind to take up those instances in which it has been translated "*appoint*" or "*ordained*" in the New Testament. Matt. xxiv. 48–51—"But and if that evil servant shall say in his heart, My lord delayeth His coming; and shall begin to smite his fellow-servants, and to eat and drink with the drunken; the Lord of that servant shall come in a day when he looketh not for Him, and in an hour that he is not aware of, and shall cut him asunder, and appoint him his portion with the hypocrites: there shall be weeping and gnashing of teeth." Here you observe that the appointment is *after* the cutting asunder, and it is the appointment of the *portion*, not of the man. The idea is most clearly that of *placing* a portion for him on the same table where that of the hypocrites is set. It is impossible to construe it into a preappointment at all. The word preserves most clearly its primary

meaning, and points out the *placing* or *setting* of the portion for the man. The same remarks apply to Luke x. 46, in which the same subject is spoken of. In John xv. 16, this same word is translated "*ordained*" as follows :—"Ye have not chosen me, but I have chosen you, and ordained you, that ye should go and bring forth fruit, and that your fruit should remain; that whatsoever ye shall ask of the Father in my name, He may give it you." This passage has been often quoted in proof of eternal choice; but reflection upon it for a moment will show, that Jesus is speaking of the choice which He made of His disciples for the purpose of the apostleship. If any doubt of this is still entertained, it will be dismissed by attention to what Jesus says Himself—John vii. 70, 71, "Jesus answered them, have not I chosen you twelve, and one of you is a devil? He spake of Judas Iscariot, the son of Simon: for he it was that should betray him, being one of the twelve." Here Jesus says that He had *chosen* Judas as well as the rest, and to understand this of eternal choice to life is absurd. He did choose him, as He chose the rest, to that office into which He actually *placed* them. He is not, then, speaking of *foreordination* in the passage before us, nor of preappointment, but of his actually *placing* His disciples in that situation in which they were to go forth to the world and bear fruit in the salvation of men. In 1 Tim. ii. 7, Paul speaks of his being "*ordained a preacher*," and he uses this word to signify his ordination—that is, his being actually *placed* in his office. He uses the *same* word in the same sense in 1 Tim. i. 12, where it is rendered "*putting* me into the ministry," and in 2 Tim. i. 11. It has manifestly the same meaning in Heb. i. 2. The word is rendered "appointed," in regard to Jesus, to signify His actual possession of all things, as it is said in another place that God the Father "hath delivered all things into His hands." These, then, are the only instances in which this word occurs, in which even our translators have given it the *slightest shade* of the meaning of an appointment before-hand; and in not one of these has it this meaning in the evident mind of the sacred writer. This will be still more evident, however, to the mind of the hearer by looking at a few of those instances in which the word is rendered according to its proper meaning. Math. v. 15, "And *put* it under a bushel;" xii. 18, "I will *put* my Spirit upon him;" xiv. 3, "and *put* him in prison;" xvii. 60, "and *laid* it in His own new tomb;" Mark vi. 56, "they *laid* the sick in the streets;" xi. 16, "He took them up in His arms, *put* His hands upon them, and blessed them;" xv. 47, "beheld where He was *laid*;" xvi. 6, "behold the place where they *laid* Him;" Luke v. 18, "and to *lay* him before them;" vi. 48, "and *laid* the foundation on a rock;" viii. 16, "or *putteth* it under a bed." It is unnecessary that I should further multiply instances. The mind of the hearer can not but be convinced from these (in which I have marked the occurrence of the word in question in italics), that it signifies not a preappointment, or foreordination, but an actual *putting* or *placing* in a particular situation, as I have already said. This will be seen to be most important in rightly understanding the passage before us.

2. *Paul then says,* "*For God hath not placed us into wrath.*" He is speaking of their situation as they stood at the time when he wrote; and it will be seen that the line of distinction which he drew, was between the believer and the unbeliever, and not between the one portion of mankind and the other, on any different principle of distinction. The grand essential of the doctrine of universal predestination, is the eternal division of men, not into believers and unbelievers, or into righteous and wicked, but into the predestinated to life and the predestinated unto death. One portion of unbelievers are on this principle regarded as *already appointed* to life, and the other to death. This division of *unbelievers* is most unscriptural; and it is especially unscriptural to include unbelievers in the appointment of life. Nothing can be clearer than this, that the Ephesian Christians before they believed, were *placed in wrath*—they " were by nature the children of wrath even as others." (Eph. ii. 3.) Nor can anything be more decisive on this subject, than the solemn declaration, " he that believeth not the Son shall not see life; but the wrath of God abideth on him," and so " He that believeth not is condemned already." The whole unreconciled and unbelieving world are placed in wrath; and this is just this condemned condition out of which the sinner is taken when he believes the gospel, and is justified of God. The statement, then, that " God hath not placed us into wrath," is the very same as the statement that " he that believeth on the Son of God is not con-

demned,"—he is not placed under the displeasure and condemnation of God. Surely, nothing can be more evident than the truth, that he who derives the idea of an eternal appointment of men to wrath from this text, derives that from it which was never in it by the intention of the apostle or of the Spirit of God.

3. *Paul says further*, "*For God hath placed us into the possession of salvation.*" Having already pointed out the meaning of the word rendered "appointed," the translation will appear clear to the mind of the hearer, so far as that word is concerned. You will observe, however, that the word rendered in the text before us, "*to obtain*," I have rendered "*possession.*" This is an undoubted meaning of the word, and is seen to be the apostle's meaning of it here by its connection with the word which means *placing*, as I have already shown. It does not appear sense at all to say—"put into the *obtaining* of salvation"—or, "placed into the *obtaining* of salvation;" whereas it is most simple and ordinary language to say—"put into the *possession* of salvation." This is the clear and simple sense of Paul's words. But it may be well to give one or two instances to prove this. In Eph. i. 14, we have the following translation of the same word: "Until the redemption of the purchased *possession.*" Here the word is rendered "possession," and can not be translated otherwise. In 1 Peter ii. 9, Christians are called "a *peculiar* people,"—in the margin "a purchased people," but most literally, "a people of *possession.*" That this, then, is a most undoubted meaning of the word, will not be

denied; and the passage before us, taken in connection with other scriptures, is thus most clear: "For God hath not placed us into wrath, but into the possession of salvation by Jesus Christ." See how this accords with other scriptures: "He that believeth on the Son of God *hath* everlasting life." Is not this most clearly declaring that he is put in possession of salvation? Is it not showing the very same truth as the text before us? Believers are already saved. "Who *hath saved* us," is the language in which they refer to Jehovah as their Lord and Redeemer. The text in hand, therefore, points out that which God did when the Thessalonian Christians believed—He placed them in the possession of salvation, so that whether they should "wake or sleep," they should live together with Jesus.

4. *Paul says that God placed them in the possession of salvation " on account of Jesus Christ."* This shows us the true ground of the salvation of those that believe. That ground is the Lord Jesus. This is a ground very different from that which is found in an eternal predestination. Jesus is "the Saviour of the world." He is the "ransom" paid "for all." "He is the propitiation for the sins of the whole world," and hence there is not a soul possessed of human nature upon the earth, that is not welcome to be placed in possession of salvation *on His account.* "WHOSOEVER believeth in Him shall not perish." "He that believeth on the Son of God hath everlasting life;" and who is not welcome so to believe? The possession of salvation spoken of in the passage before us, as "through," or "on account of" Jesus, is evidently on account

of His death, for it is immediately added, "Who died for us." Now, this ground is equally good to all, for Paul shows most unhesitatingly that Jesus did die for all (2 Cor. v. 14). O! my hearer, turn not aside from this glorious truth, as if it concerned others, and did not concern you. Let me entreat you to study this precious passage, and know, and rejoice to know, that Jesus died for you, and that on His account you are as truly welcome to salvation as any soul that ever was saved.

II. LET US NOTICE SOME OF THE IMPORTANT TRUTHS THAT ARE INVOLVED IN THIS APPOINTMENT OF GOD.

From what we have already seen, it is clear the appointment is Jehovah's placing the soul of the believer in a state of safety. This is the leading idea of the passage, but it is associated with many other truths.

1. *We are here taught that believers are already saved.* They are already in *possession* of everlasting life. How many there are who look upon the salvation of the soul as an event only to take place at death, if it take place at all. Hence they seize upon the words expressed in the verse preceding that in which we are chiefly concerned—"the hope of salvation"—and they look upon the "*hope*" that they will yet be saved as all that is required. They are content thus to hang in dark suspense between heaven and hell. They overlook the truth, that "the hope of salvation" is the hope that belongs to salvation—the hope which is wrapt up in salvation

—the hope which a man possesses when he has been put into possession of salvation. This is clearly the meaning of the apostle in the passage before us. They had the hope because they were saved. It was not the hope of being saved, but the hope of meeting their Judge in peace and safety, because they were already put in possession of salvation. To see this, you have only to consult the connection of the apostle's words. Hear what he says in verses 1–5—" But of the times and the seasons, brethren, ye have no need that I write unto you. For yourselves know perfectly, that the day of the Lord so cometh as a thief in the night. For when they shall say, Peace and safety, then sudden destruction cometh upon them, as travail upon a woman with child; and they shall not escape. But ye, brethren, are not in darkness, that that day should overtake you as a thief. Ye are all the children of light, and the children of the day; we are not of the night, nor of darkness." Here he tells them that they *are* " children of the day," and speaks to them without the slightest reserve as saved persons. My hearer, are you saved? Are you in *possession* of life? Say not that you do not know whether you are or not. This is absurd. Life is not so small a matter but, if you do possess it, you will know. Have you peace with God? Are you ready for the day that shall come suddenly upon the unbeliever? You must know if you are ready. You must know if you would have felt *yourself* included in Paul's description, had you heard him saying to certain persons, " Ye are children of the day." I beseech you, do not lower the blessedness of the state of a believer, merely that it may suit your own experience. No, rather let your false hope perish at once, than have it sustained in such a way. To be a Christian, is to be in possession of safety.

2. *We are taught, in this passage, that believers are put in possession of salvation* ON ACCOUNT OF JESUS CHRIST. Now you may have been accustomed to regard this as a settled truth, from your earliest years; and yet you may never have seen its true extent. You may have been all the time acting and feeling as if sinners were saved on account of their *faith*, or on account of their *holiness*. As an evidence of this, observe, that you have no idea that Jesus can ever be better that He is, as a ground on which to justify the sinner. You think that you know Jesus as He is, and you wish to be justified and put in possession of safety. But you are not justified. You have no peace or you have no safety. You think you have Jesus, and that His atonement is sufficient so far as it goes; but it does not go far enough to save you. And yet you do believe. You do not doubt the truth of the gospel —and still you are not saved. Why is it thus with you? Because you think your faith is not as it should be, or your love is not as it should be. If these were fully rectified, and perfect, then you think you would be saved. O! my friend, you are not thinking of being put in possession of safety on account of Christ at all, but on account of your own goodness, as faith, or love, or holiness. See to it well, for God will place no man in possession of salvation on any other ground but on that of the

finished satisfaction for sin given by Jesus on Calvary.

3. *We are informed here of a salvation that is free to every man.* Had it been said that God had put them in possession of salvation, on account of His eternal decree, by which He had separated them from the rest of mankind, then, the idea of this salvation being free to all, would be the very height of absurdity. But this is not said. They were not put in possession of salvation on account of an eternal decree of this nature, but on account of the death of Jesus. Had it been said that they were put in possession of salvation by an influence of the Spirit, which was destined from eternity to be used only with a small portion of men, then the idea of the salvation being free to all would be out of the question. Or had it been said, that they were put in possession of salvation on account of a change produced in them by this specially destined influence, the same conclusion would follow. Or, to pass to another barrier—had it been said that they were put in possession of salvation because of their own holiness or goodness, then there would have been no access *for all* to the situation in which they stood. But rejoice, my hearer, and seek to make the hearts of others rejoice too, they were put in possession of safety, on account of a great sacrifice that was made *for you as much as for them*, and that has been accepted for you as truly as for them; and, on the ground of it, you are as welcome to approach God, and to be put in possession of this salvation, as ever they were. Hear his own words: " Look unto me, and be ye saved, all ye ends of the

earth; for I am God, and besides me there is none else."

4. *We learn from the exposition of this passage how needlessly the mind of the inquiring sinner has been encumbered with the doctrine of predestination.* That doctrine has been made to stand forth before him, wherever, by the utmost stretch of Scripture language, it could be made to find the slightest shadow of support. How many eyes have grown dim, with soul-destroying embarrassment, in poring over this same passage. The inquiring and guilty sinner has thought of the immense value and necessity of an appointment to be saved—a decree on his behalf fixing his destiny for heaven. He has also been made to tremble and shudder with inward horror at the idea of his being appointed to wrath by the inexorable determination of God; and, blinded with this idea, he has sought in vain for rest and refuge in the truth contained in the Bible. How strange that he should have been looking upon one of the plainest passages in that book, and one speaking as plainly as possible of salvation for him. For, it is most clear that since God put Paul and the Thessalonians in possession of safety on account of Jesus who died for them, the same ground avails for every other sinner for whom Jesus died. Yes, my hearer, it is not only true that this ground is as good for you as it was for them; but also that Jehovah's most earnest desire is, that you would consent to be justified, and so put in possession of this salvation, on the same ground. And when He justifies, who shall condemn? When He tells you to be at peace for the sake of such an atonement, who

shall make you afraid? And when He puts you in *possession* of salvation, is not your security great indeed? Come near, then, to the throne of your God, with nothing but the finished atonement of Jesus as your plea, and you must be saved.

LECTURE XVII.

PREDESTINATION AS A FOUNDATION OF HOPE.

In this, our closing lecture, attention will be chiefly directed to 2 Timothy ii. 19:—"Nevertheless the foundation of the Lord standeth sure, having this seal, The Lord knoweth them that are His. And, let every one that nameth the name of Christ depart from iniquity." This text is supposed to teach the doctrine of predestination very strongly. It is quoted in the Confession of Faith as one proof of the "passing by," or eternal abandonment of those who are not among the elect. Cruden says, "*God's decree of election is the firm, immovable foundation upon which the salvation of the elect depends.*" This same idea is strong in the minds of many others. The following passages will show this. The one is from an old, the other is from a living author:—"In ascribing the salvation of the remnant of the people to the election of grace, Paul clearly testifies, that it is there only known that God saves whom He will of His mere good pleasure, and does not dispense a reward to which there can be no claim. They who shut the gates to prevent any one from presuming to approach and taste this doctrine, do no less injury to man than to God; for nothing else will be sufficient to produce in us suitable humility, or to impress us with a due sense of our great obligations to God. Nor is there any other basis for solid confidence, even according to the authority of Christ, who, to deliver us from fear, and render us invincible amidst so many dangers, snares, and deadly conflicts, promises to preserve in safety all whom the Father hath committed to His care. Whence we infer, that they who know not themselves to be God's peculiar people, will be tortured with continual anxiety; and therefore, that the interest of all the faithful as well as their own, is very badly consulted by those who, blind to the three advantages we have remarked, would wholly remove the foundation of our salvation."* Nothing can be clearer than that Calvin looked upon this doctrine of predestination as the very resting-place of the soul. The following words show that such an idea is not yet extinct:—" And finally, to pass from the present scene of trial to the future world of blessedness and glory, how unmeaning, on any theory of universal reference in the atonement, does the song of the countless multitude before the throne become! Then we see the mighty mystery of God's will accomplished, even the purpose which He hath purposed in Himself— 'that in the dispensation of the fullness of times He might gather together in one all things in Christ, both which are in heaven, and which are on earth; even in Him.' (Eph. i. 10.) One universal family or household is gathered together, out of every kindred, and people, and nation, and tongue; and the note of praise which, as they sing the new song, they all with united voices give forth, is but one

* Calvin's Inst., book iii. chap. xxi.

continued acknowledgment of special obligation to the Lamb for His death—and for His death as exclusively on their behalf; otherwise, it could not be any special ground of thanksgiving, which they make it, when they salute their Saviour with the adoring hymn:—'Thou art worthy; for thou wast slain, and hast redeemed us to God by thy blood.'"* It is most clear, then, that Calvin thought, that if we removed the doctrine of predestination, we removed the foundation of hope; and that Dr. Candlish thinks, that if we remove it, we deprive the song of heaven itself of all its glory! If the saved are not enabled to look upon themselves as the *exclusive favorites*, all is lost! No wonder, when men think thus of the doctrine of predestination, that they cling to it as with the determination of a death grasp. This fact, however, makes it a very important duty in us to search into the truth, both as regards the foundation of hope, and the theme of the heavenly song. It bids us see to it, whether we can not trust to the Saviour, if *all* have a place in His heart, and an atonement made for them in His finished work, and whether we shall not be able to sing His praise as having died for us, if it turn out to be true that He died for all.

I. Let us consider the doctrine of predestination as a foundation of hope for man.

The doctrine itself is already before the hearer; it is, that a certain portion of men are infallibly predestinated to heaven, and the rest "passed by"

* Candlish on the Atonement, p. 46.

and abandoned to the suffering of eternal woe. Now, this doctrine appears deficient in two aspects —first, it is deficient when viewed as a resting-place upon which hopes are already founded; and, second, it is deficient when viewed as a ground upon which to ask sinners to found their hopes. We shall consider it in both of these aspects.

1. *Consider this doctrine as a foundation already rested on.* It is not necessary to look to the doctrine itself as the *only* rest, because those from whom we have quoted make Jesus their rest; but they seem to be unable to rest upon Him, unless they are permitted to view Him in the light of a predestination that includes some and altogether excludes others. It is, therefore, in this light that I desire to view their ground of assurance and peace.

(1.) Predestination, as understood by those whose views we are now considering, grievously darkens the LOVE of God. Mark, my hearer, many who have been trained as Christians, and have thought themselves of the "*elect*," have abandoned Christianity altogether; and that not for want of thought, but because they did *think* on their system. It is not long since a most thoughtful and intelligent man told me, that he had been led to abandon all the hopes he had formerly entertained of heaven, because when he began to *reflect* upon the *character* of the God he had been trusting, he found that to be the character of a capricious tyrant, and not that of a Father or of a God. Mark well, my hearer, you may yet yourself come to reflect upon the real nature of the "*grace*" you are trusting;

and if you find that it is such as to include one and to exclude another, for no reason but because it so pleases Him whose grace it is, you may begin to think that this *can not* be God. Do not be too confident. If you are trusting to a grace that is thus partial,—most unaccountably partial—there is a *flaw* in the idea upon which your soul is leaning, and you are not beyond the possibility of yet concluding that this idea is a falsehood—an ungodlike falsehood; and you may yet be exposed to the gulf into which others have plunged before you: when renouncing a partial God they *thought* they had cast off Jehovah. I do therefore press the truth, that the doctrine of predestination, as we have now to do with it—a predestination of some to life and of others to death before they were born—is a *flaw* in the ground of hope of him who entertains it, instead of being a principle of strength. It is that which makes *every one* who adopts it take shelter in mystery or doubt, and too often in confirmed skepticism. It is not an easy matter for the soul of a reflecting man to rest upon *partial* love.

(2.) But this doctrine is injurious to the ground of hope, because it calls for something additional to the Word of God that the sinner may have confidence. The doctrine itself implies that no man can find his part in Christ Jesus simply by means of the Bible. There he can find that God loves *some* men —that Jesus atoned for *some* men—that the Holy Spirit is predestinated for *some* men; but according to this doctrine it is not possible that he can find in the Bible alone the truth that this great salvation is for him. If he finds this at all, he must find it somewhere else than in the Bible. "Heaven and earth shall pass away" but "the word of the Lord abideth for ever." This is a glorious truth, so far as it shows that there is salvation for some men, but it can not, on the doctrine in question, show any sinner that there is salvation for him. He must turn in some other direction, and in millions of instances men do turn in some other direction, to find that Jesus died for them. Ask a man who holds this doctrine, if he is one of those for whom Jesus died. It may be, he will answer, "Yes." Ask him, then, how he knows that Jesus died for him: he can not answer—"From the Bible alone." He does not believe that Jesus died for all, and the Bible does not contain a list of the "elect"—he must go somewhere else for his answer. It is impossible, on this doctrine, for any one to believe with Paul ("He loved me and gave Himself for me"), without going for that faith to some other source than the simple and unchanging record of God's word. Hear the following description of assurance :—" Seeing Christ with the new eye which the Spirit purges, grasping him with the new hand which the Spirit strengthens, believing all the Divine testimony with that clear intelligence which belongs to the renewed mind, and that eager consent which the renewed heart hastens to give—I am Christ's, and Christ is mine; I am become a partaker of the divine nature ; for as Christ is so am I."* Now let us ask the person who expresses himself thus—how do you know that Christ is yours? Where must he go for the reply? Sup-

* Dr. Candlish on the Atonement.

pose we ask him, How do you know that Jesus died for you? Where must he go for a reply? It is impossible he can go to the Bible. That book, according to his doctrine, contains no answer to these questions. What, then, is the ground of his hope and assurance? It can not be the unfailing word of God.

(3.) This doctrine of the predestination of some to life and of others to death, leads the soul to rest upon its own changeable feelings. What, for example, is meant by such expressions as these:—" Seeing Christ with a new eye "—" grasping Christ with a new hand "—" cleaving to Christ with a new heart." What *facts* of human consciousness do they express or represent? Let us not be led away with mere figures of speech. Whatever these facts be, they are the facts upon which the sinner is expected to ground his confidence and the belief that Jesus died for him. Now what are these facts? If you, my hearer, are resting in Christ because these facts have taken place with you—if you believe that you are predestinated to glory because you " see Christ with a new eye," what do you mean by this " new eye?" It must be something that can bear a plain designation. What, then, is it? I answer for you—It is merely a *new feeling* of your own mind. It is not—it can not be a part of the Word of God. You would not call that " a new eye." Mark, then, the only answer you can give to the question—How do you know that Jesus died for you?—is, that you have a *feeling* which you had not before, and which you think the " reprobate " can not possibly have. It just comes to this, then, that your only ground of hope is a *feeling* of your own mind. Take away this—let the "new eye" be darkened, and your hope is gone; let the "new hand" be paralyzed, and your hope is gone; and you can not have recourse to the Bible for its renewal, for you did not get it there at first: you must wait for the "new eye," or more simply, the "new feeling," to arise once more. O! it is deeply grievous to think how many are in deep and Bible-neglecting delusion from this cause. They have long ago come to the conclusion, that Jesus died for none but a selected number; they have left the Bible as a book that can not possibly give them any assurance of their safety in meeting God, and they are sometimes up, sometimes down, as their *changeable* feelings fluctuate.

(4.) This doctrine is injurious to the foundation of hope, inasmuch as it contradicts one of the plainest truths of the Bible. How is it possible to express a truth in plainer language than this: "God so loved THE WORLD that He delivered up His only-begotten Son, that whosoever believeth in Him should not perish but have everlasting life?" So, "there is one God, and one Mediator between God and man, the man Christ Jesus, who gave Himself A RANSOM FOR ALL;" and thus "He is the propitiation for our sins, and not for ours only, but also for the sins of THE WHOLE WORLD." Here, my dear hearer, is ground enough for you to approach the throne of God as a dark, cold, vile, guilty wretch, with the perfect assurance that you will be accepted; and so here is ground enough for the Christian to rest on in *his* darkest hour. But what havoc does the doctrine now before us make of this ground of confidence! It tells you that the world for whom God surrendered His own Son, is not the whole world of men; that the "all" for whom Jesus gave Himself a ransom is "not all men;" nay, that "the whole world" is not "the whole world," but a small portion of it, predestinated to life from all eternity, while "the rest" are abandoned to perish in their sins! This takes the firm and solid rock from beneath the feet of the Christian himself, and leaves him to scramble back to his own good experiences, that he may count himself among "the elect." Let me beseech you, my hearer, to reflect upon your own assurance: see if it does not consist simply in your feelings; see that it has the changeless WORD OF GOD to rely on, or you may find it a sad matter for your soul in the hour of trial.

2. *Let us now consider the doctrine in hand, as offering rest to the guilty.* I shall do this more briefly, as what I have said will open the way to that which I have now to say.

(1.) Consider the character in which man is justified and accepted of God. He "justifieth the *ungodly.*" It is when looking upon himself as "ungodly," that the sinner, believing, is justified. Take the case of the publican in the temple. He looked upon himself as ungodly—nothing but a sinner—when he was justified. The Pharisee looked upon himself as godly, and he was condemned. There is nothing that can exceed the importance of this truth; and it is just turned upside down by the doctrine I have been opposing. The sinner must find that he has a "new heart," that is, a *godly heart*, before he can *think* that Jesus died for him; and it is impossible he can be justified before he believes this truth. O! my hearer, is it not your own idea, that you can not be justified until you get a new heart?

(2.) Consider the absolute necessity of "appropriation," as it is called, in order to the justification of the soul. By appropriation, is meant the belief of the mind that Jesus atoned for its own sins—that which is expressed in the words—"He died for me." On all hands this must be regarded as necessary to salvation. It is not difficult to see how the redeemed can rejoice in Jesus, though they see that He was a ransom for others as well as for them; but it is *impossible* to read their song without the word "*us*," containing for the individual mind the word "*me*," "who loved me and gave Himself for me." No man has the faith by which Paul was saved, who is not prepared so to speak of Jesus. Well, here is just the point when the doctrine in question throws in its huge barrier. You may speak of the completeness of Jesus' work in terms of angelic description. If you can not on God's authority tell me that this work was undertaken and finished for me—how is my faith in what you say to lead me to express myself with Paul? It can do no such thing, and hence that appropriation to myself, being absolutely necessary to my peace, you send me away to my feelings for authority to appropriate!

It is important to observe also that this doctrine is most certainly injurious when the mind is fully disposed to reflect honestly and solemnly on the ground of its hope for eternity. In a certain state of mind, a man may swallow the grossest absurdities, simply because he is not at all scrupulous whether he believe truth or error. When a man *reflects* deeply, this is the state of mind in which he is inevitably stumbled by the doctrine of predestination. To show the vast importance of this truth, it is not long since I spoke with a man who, when young, had been what he believed to be a Christian. He got acquainted with some infidels. He thought it his duty to make an effort to turn them to the truth; but ere long he found that he had *taken for granted* the very foundations of his own belief, and that these proved contradictions when reflected on, and tested, as he found them tested, by the arguments of his fellow-workmen. He was speedily plunged in infidelity with the rest; but neither could his inquiring and reflecting mind rest here. Though he felt no ground in his former belief, he found as little in having no belief at all, and it was after years of anxious, and after agonizing inquiry, that his mind rested on the truth of the Bible, seen in John iii. 16. This is the state of mind, then, in which a man refuses to trust to his own feelings, and is debarred from trusting to the finished work of Jesus, by the doctrine now in question.

II. LET US NOW CONSIDER THE FOUNDATION MENTIONED IN THE PASSAGE BEFORE US.

Having shown the evil effects of predestination, not only as a foundation itself, but in its influence upon the foundation truly laid, it is most important that we now see the real foundation as viewed by the apostle in the text in hand.

1. *Let us consider the foundation itself.* This is mentioned in several other passages of the Bible under this particular figure. Isaiah xxviii. 16— "Therefore, thus saith the Lord God, Behold I lay in Zion for a foundation, a stone, a tried stone, a precious corner-stone, a sure foundation; he that believeth shall not make haste." This passage is quoted and distinctly applied to Jesus at length in 1 Peter ii. 6. The same is very distinctly stated in 1 Corinthians iii. 10, 11—"According to the grace of God which is given unto me, as a wise master-builder, I have laid the foundation, and another buildeth thereon. But let every man take heed how he buildeth thereupon. For other foundation can no man lay than that is laid, which is Jesus Christ." Jesus Christ, then, is the foundation of God; and when the apostle says that He laid the foundation, he refers simply to his proclamation of Jesus. What, then, are we to understand by Jesus as a foundation? In answering this question, we must remember that *minds* are built on Jesus. Now, how do minds rest upon a foundation? By confiding in it. Confidence is just the *leaning* of the soul, and from this arises the structure of hopes which are raised above the foundation on which the confidence is rested. It will be seen immediately that Jesus, as proclaimed by Paul, is a foundation very different from that which is furnished by predestination; but it is most important to see clearly that a foundation for the mind is simply that on

which the mind may rest with intelligent confidence—that in view of which all fear and trembling are dismissed, and are superseded by the firm unshaken trust of the soul—that by which man is intelligently and most reasonably *assured* that the bosom of his God is open for him, as the heart of the prodigal's father was for his returning son—that in view of which the sinner actually goes to a throne of grace sure of welcome, and hopes to go to a throne of judgment in perfect safety. Jesus Christ is this foundation, so that "he that believeth in Him shall not be confounded." It is most important, then, to see whether Paul leaned upon this foundation as one limited to the accommodation of only some men, or as actually laid for all. This will be infallibly seen from his own words. When, then, he came among the Corinthians, and laid this foundation at Corinth first, how did he speak? He tells us himself. "Christ died for our sins according to the scriptures, and was buried, and rose again the third day, according to the scriptures." This he declares to have been the "*gospel*" which he first of all preached to them. How could any man of all his hearers understand by this, that Jesus died only for some of them? Only think, my hearer, if you had been one of Paul's audience, and you had heard him at the very first, before there was a single Christian at Corinth besides himself, declaring that Jesus died for "our" sins, would you not have understood yourself as included in this "our?" Paul had manifestly no idea of limitation. No; his soul burned to preach the gospel to "every creature," because he knew that it contained a *solid* ground of confidence and hope for every creature whose ears it could reach. But we are not left even with this. Paul tells us in another place how he believed in Jesus. 2 Cor. v. 14, 15 :—" For the love of Christ constraineth us, because we thus judge." Now, how did he judge? Did he decide in his mind that Jesus had only died for some men? Read his own words:—" We thus judge, that if one died for all, then were all dead; and that He died for all, that they who live "—(Who were these?—"*they who live*"—most assuredly they who are raised from among the " all " that are dead —that is, believers)—" might not live unto themselves, but unto Him who died for them and rose again." "They who live," are manifestly *a part* only of those for whom Jesus died. How is it *possible* for any man to fail in perceiving that, when Paul laid the foundation at Corinth, it was in the all-embracing gospel of the death of Jesus for the life of the world. Here, then, my hearer, is the foundation. Is it not broad enough for you? Is it not firm enough for you? There are those who tell you that if it be an atonement for all, it is no ground of confidence for any—are you of this mind? Then remember this, you differ essentially from him who declared that Jesus did die for all, and yet gloried in the cross as far more than sufficient for him. Mark especially, that in the foundation thus viewed there is nothing required but Jesus to give you eternal confidence. Since God is satisfied with His work of expiation, and satisfied for you, and ready to receive you on this ground, as a poor, guilty sinner, and as such only, there is no room for your leaving this foundation to build on your possession of a "new eye," or on your grasping with a "new hand," or your cleaving with a "new heart." All as you are, you are atoned for by the accursed death being suffered in your stead, and you are most heartily welcome to look up and say Abba, Father, to your God, for His heart and His hand are stretched forth to you in peace and mercy. He stands by the sacrifice—one hand rests upon the Lamb in token of righteous and honorable satisfaction with that atonement, and the other is extended to you, while He says, "Come and let us reason together, though your sins be as scarlet, they shall be as white as snow." O! my hearer, if *this* be not *ground* of confidence, what can be so? And mark well, this is unchangeable ground. This rock is not like the ever-shifting sands of your own feelings and experiences—this is unchangeable as God, for it is just His changeless love, and the changeless propitiation on account of which you are called upon to dismiss your fears. It is love to you as *a sinner*. It is an atonement *for your sins*. It is welcome to the prodigal before he has got the ring on his hand, or shoes on his feet, for it is after he has been clasped to the bosom of his forgiving Father that these are given him. He is accepted, joyfully accepted, all as he is, in the wretchedness of a prodigal, on the ground that all his sins are borne by another.

2. *Let us now consider the inscription that is seen on this foundation.* This consists of the two sentences—"The Lord knoweth them that are His," and "Let every one that nameth the name of

Christ depart from iniquity." The word rendered "seal" in the passage before us has not only this meaning, but also that of the impression made by the seal (see Rev. ix. 4), and that is equivalent to "inscription" in this case. Paul, therefore, sets the gospel of Jesus, and thus Jesus Himself before our minds, under the figure of a foundation-stone with this inscription. Thus, no one can lean upon the foundation without being aware of these two great truths. The figure is beautiful and striking. It is that of a stone on which the believer is led to build his all for time and eternity; and when first he approaches this stone, he can not but read upon it the plain legible inscription that stares him in the face. In plain language, he can not trust in Jesus without knowing these two things. It is most clear, then, that these must be truths of the very greatest moment. Let us attend to them in their order.

(1.) "*The Lord knoweth them that are His.*" This is the part of the passage in which the doctrine of a secret and eternal election is supposed to be taught. One thing, however, is fatal to this idea, and it is this:—It involves the notion that a man may be Christ's before he believes the gospel. It proceeds on the assumption that many of those *known* by the Lord as "HIS," are yet full of the spirit of the world, and led captive by Satan at his will. This is an inseparable and self-destructive part of the doctrine of predestination or election to faith. It brings the doctrine into perpetual collision with the Bible. "If any man have not the spirit of Christ, *he is none of His.*" How, in the face of such a declaration can we believe that those are His, and known as His, who are now "children of wrath," and "fulfilling the desires of the flesh?" How can the phrase,—"The Lord knoweth them that are His" be extended beyond the number of those who have the Spirit of Christ? It is impossible to do so without a direct contradiction of the Bible. Let us read the inscription according to this truth, that those only who have the spirit of Jesus are His, and the idea of an election separating two masses of men by an eternal decree, disappears entirely from the text before us. It does not leave even a shadow behind. This is in perfect accordance with the other scriptures where the same sentiment occurs. Neh. i. 7—"And He knoweth them that trust in Him." Also, Num. xvi. 5—"And He spake unto Korah, and to all his company, saying, Even to-morrow, the Lord will show who are His, and who are holy." This is rendered by the Septuagint:—"The Lord will *know* (or acknowledge) who are His, and who are holy." We may also clearly learn from these passages the great object of such an inscription upon the foundation stone of the spiritual temple. In Num. xvi. the event recorded is a contention between the servants of God and those of Satan, in which the latter claimed to be the true servants of Jehovah. This was just what Paul was engaged with when he wrote to Timothy. Two of the servants of the great deceiver had risen up in the garb of the Christian profession, and they opposed the apostle, and overthrew the faith of some. What was the apostle's firm consolation? "The Lord knoweth them that are His." He stood in the very position of

Moses with the company of Korah; and he had the very same confidence that the Lord knew and would acknowledge those who had His Spirit, and stood in reality on His side. The same truth is most strikingly manifested in Nahum i. 7, 8—"The Lord is good, a stronghold in the day of trouble: and He knoweth them that trust in Him. But with an over-running flood He will make an utter end of the place thereof, and darkness shall pursue His enemies."

Here it is most clear that the great end of the truth, which the apostle says is inscribed on the great foundation, is to convince men that nothing that is false in their professions will stand with God. How important, my hearer, then, is this inscription! How apt are men only to pretend to rest in Jesus! The apostle brings all such up to the test of an Omniscient eye, and assures them of the fundamental truth, that their pretenses and their professions are vain; and, moreover, he gives the true ground of rest and peace to the Christian when opposed by the false professor. The combat may appear doubtful. Many may be led away from the truth, and may do as those did whose faith was overthrown in the days of Paul. It may seem, as if for a time, that error has the mastery, but the Lord knows and will acknowledge them that are His. This is' most manifestly the force and aim of Paul's language, and no one can look at it in its proper light, without seeing the immense difference between it and the cold and icy fixtures of universal predestination. All are welcome to Jesus, and when truly and honestly yielded to Him, every one has the full force of this blessed inscription to bear him up in every trial.

(2.) "*Let every one who names the name of Christ depart from iniquity.*" Such is the remaining portion of the inscription which is seen upon that foundation which is laid in Zion. No one can truly approach the cross without feeling that there is no sympathy between Jesus and sin. No man ever yet truly knew the Saviour and continued in iniquity. "He that saith, I know Him, and keepeth not His commandments, is a liar." Such is the strong and solemn declaration of the word of God. Most assuredly, therefore, is it impossible for any one to lean on this tried stone without being separated from iniquity. My dear hearer, let me faithfully and kindly ask you to ponder this part of the inscription upon the foundation of human hope. Remember there is no rest in Jesus' atonement which is consistent with the continuance in what you know to be wrong. If you are in such a course, depend upon it you are not resting upon Jesus, the Son of God, the Saviour of the world—you may have rest, but it is not rest on Him.

I come, then, to a close, and once more press the great general truth upon the mind of my hearer, that you are as free to the love of your God at this moment, as the utmost welcome of His heart of love can possibly make you. As God the Father, Jehovah has loved you from eternity, and in spite of all your sins He loves you still. As the Son, He hath borne your curse, so that "*come*" is the language of justice now as well as that of mercy. As the Holy Spirit, He has condescended to plead and strive with you, that He might fix your eye upon the glorious liberty provided for you by the death of Jesus. Not a decree that ever He passed is against your now entering into peace with your kind and propitiated God—all, all is free. All combine to draw you with the cords of love: "The Spirit and the Bride say, Come—and let him that heareth say, Come—and let him that is athirst come —and whosoever will, let him take the water of life freely."

THE END.

www.ingramcontent.com/pod-product-compliance
Lightning Source LLC
Chambersburg PA
CBHW031330230426
43670CB00006B/302